MICHEL ODENT

Water and Sexuality

ARKANA

ARKANA

Published by the Penguin Group
27 Wrights Lane, London w8 5TZ, England
Viking Penguin Inc., 40 West 23rd Street, New York, New York 10010, USA
Penguin Books Australia Ltd, Ringwood, Victoria, Australia
Penguin Books Canada Ltd, 2801 John Street, Markham, Ontario, Canada L3R 1B4
Penguin Books (NZ) Ltd, 182–190 Wairau Road, Auckland 10, New Zealand

Penguin Books Ltd, Registered Offices: Harmondsworth, Middlesex, England

First published 1990

Copyright © Michel Odent, 1990

The lines from Heathcote Williams's *Whale Nation* (Jonathan Cape, 1988)
on p. 63 and *Falling for a Dolphin* (Jonathan Cape, 1988) on p. 96
are quoted by kind permission of the author and the publishers

Made and printed in Great Britain by
Richard Clay Ltd, Bungay, Suffolk
Filmset in 10 on 12pt Monophoto Sabon

The name of Dr Michel Odent is associated worldwide with birth under water.

Michel Odent was an overworked surgeon, doing mostly emergency surgery, which included Caesarean births. He began to question how Caesareans could be prevented and as a result of his researches developed the maternity unit in Pithiviers Hospital, France. This seemingly insignificant place became a focal point for the new consciousness surrounding the subject of birth. He wanted to know more about what home birth could offer and undertook the work of a midwife. He is author of *Entering the World*, *Genèse de l'homme écologique*, *Birth Reborn*, *Primal Health* and co-author of *The Z Factor*.

Water and Sexuality

To make *Homo 'sapiens'* better understood,
Wilhelm Reich turned our eyes
towards new-born babies and the desert.
This book is dedicated to him –
the great sexologist of this century.

Contents

Contents

LIST OF ILLUSTRATIONS

ACKNOWLEDGEMENTS

I owe special thanks to my son Pascal, who gave his mummy Judy Graham enough freedom to translate my Franglais into genuine English.

Special thanks to Alice Charlwood, who also helped me to put some chapters into good English, and to Muriel Tristant who typed nearly everything.

INTRODUCTION

For many thousands of years the countless philosophers and scholars who pronounced on human nature did so without seeing that man is first an aquatic primate. The time has come for a radically new vision of man.

I became aware of the power of water in a surprising way and in an unexpected environment. In a French state hospital in Pithiviers, where I was in charge of the surgical unit, I practised all kinds of emergency surgery, including Caesareans. As I was a rather overworked surgeon, my main aim was to reduce the number of operations I was called on to perform. When it came to Caesareans, I questioned whether it might be possible to make labour easier. I considered the effects of the environment on the birth process. As my original training had not been as an obstetrician, I did not try to find the answer in books. In any case, textbooks would not have provided the solution. Instead, I learned from the women who came to give birth and from the midwives.

It soon became apparent that many women wanted to take a shower or a bath during labour. But what I found really interesting was the incredible attraction to water that some had while in labour. So, at the maternity unit at the hospital in Pithiviers, we responded to what the women seemed to need. First of all, as a temporary measure, we had a big plastic paddling pool that could be filled with warm water. Later on we installed a very large, round, deep-blue bath that was plumbed in.

I had a revelation the day a woman gave birth on the floor before the pool was actually full. All she needed was to *see* the blue water. Until that moment I had only physiological explanations as to why warm water helped during labour. But this particular woman helped me to go beyond such simplistic thoughts. For the first time I was able to see the importance of water as a symbol and the role it can play in human sexuality.

We all went through another stage the day a mother-to-be did not feel the need to leave the bath at the time of the birth. The baby was born under water, like a dolphin. Many journalists with a nose for a story were excited by the news of birth taking place under water. Why? This question prompted me to study more thoroughly the relationship between humans and water.

During this study the word 'sexuality' took on an even broader meaning, going far beyond the mere genitalia, and farther still beyond events of sexual life such as giving birth and breast-feeding. Sexuality emerges as the very opposite of a copying process, quite the reverse of reproduction. It is based on new combinations of pre-existing genes. Sexuality implies creativity. Inversely, there is something sexual in a creative process. Human creativity is based on new combinations of preformulated ideas. In a sexualized world, the future is always different from the present. When one is endowed with human consciousness, sexuality also means an interest in the future, a concern for future generations. It is the capacity not to confuse one's own death with the end of the universe. That is why this book is also about humanity's ability to disturb profoundly the natural cycle of water, at the risk of destroying life on the planet. And, finally, it holds out the vision of an authentic *Homo sapiens*.

CHAPTER 1

How to Use Water During Labour

Anecdotes

A pregnant woman had but one obsession: to give birth under water. She threw herself with great energy into realizing her dream. In the end some friends lent her their home: a comfortable flat with a huge bath. On the day of the delivery, the mother-to-be was coming and going between the toilet and the bedroom, shouting out without restraint, as is common during a fast labour. Before long, she gave birth to her baby on the carpet by the bed. Two hours later, having held the baby close to her the entire time, she suddenly came back down to earth and said, 'By the way, I forgot the bath!'

Another young woman travelled thousands of miles to use the small pool in the maternity unit at Pithiviers Hospital. She was a diver and was in her element in water. But on the day of the birth she made only a short appearance in the pool.

Another woman, living locally in the heart of the town, had never before been in a swimming-pool; she could not swim and used to claim that she would have nothing to do with such tricks. However, on the day of the birth, she was irresistibly attracted by the water and could not leave the bath before the birth of her baby.

There are no simple formulas for the use of water during labour. It is not a method that can be evaluated by 'double blind' studies. The attraction to water during labour varies considerably from one woman to another. It can be neither measured nor forecast. There is no parallel with an attraction to water in daily life.

Practical Advice

I have learned from experience that there are a number of rules for the beneficial use of water during labour. By following these guidelines, I have no doubt that a contribution can be made towards controlling the epidemic of Caesareans that has insidiously invaded the industrialized world.

There are few hospitals where the importance to labouring women of privacy, darkness and silence, of a feminine environment, of the freedom to move and to be noisy, are all taken into consideration. But even in these hospitals some modern women still find it difficult to release all their inhibitions. In other words, they are unable to liberate their instincts. Water can be a help.

Ideally, the pool should be large enough to allow the woman to adopt any position and deep enough to make complete immersion possible. If it is overly large, too much time is required to fill and empty it, and once full, the atmosphere of privacy is reduced. A similar problem can arise if the pool is constructed in a transparent material. A round pool with a diameter of around 2 metres and a depth of 70 centimetres or so is a perfect size. The room itself should be as small as possible. The prevailing colours should be considered. Light blue reinforces an aquatic atmosphere. When pregnant women dream of water, it is always a brilliant blue.

For practical reasons it is difficult to add salt so as to reproduce the density of sea water. We have tried, but it takes time to dissolve a stone or more of salt, and it is expensive.

Still in a practical vein, the pipes should be large enough so that it does not take too long to fill and empty the tub. The water must be constantly regulated and kept at body temperature.

When a woman gets into the bath during labour, it often has a spectacular effect for the first hour. Simple observations of this kind are the key to the best use of water in childbirth.

If a mother-to-be goes to the bath before the onset of hard labour, the contractions may stop. On the other hand, the cervix may dilate several centimetres quite rapidly. However, this will not necessarily prevent the protraction of the later stages of labour. Alternatively, if the mother-to-be gets into the water only when hard labour is established and when the dilation of the cervix is well advanced (for example, at least 5 centimetres), the end of the first stage can be very fast: in the region of one hour for a first baby.

On entering the pool, the mother often gives a great sigh, expressing relief and even well-being. After that, rapid dilation is often accompanied by what might be called a deep regression. She cuts herself off from our world, forgetting what she has learned, what she has read, all her received ideas. She dares to shout out without restraint, and loses control of her breathing and position. Well-intentioned attendants should become less and less intrusive, as her inner trip takes her deeper and deeper. It is as if the water were protecting her from useless stimuli.

If the midwife is familiar with birth in an atmosphere of intimacy and spontaneity, she has no need to disturb the birth process with vaginal examinations. Even from the next room she will know what is happening: she has only to listen. She can assess the stage of labour according to how fast, how deeply and how noisily the woman is breathing. The midwife can also sense when the labour has stopped and when the contractions are no longer efficient. It often means that the baby is not far away.

If the contractions suddenly stop being efficient, the mother also feels it. If she trusts what she feels, if she is not a prisoner of a project in terms of giving birth under water, she does not hesitate to leave the bath right away.

Getting Out of the Water before the Birth

Leaving the warm water and returning to a cooler atmosphere often triggers off one, two or three irresistible contractions – and the baby is born.

No two births are the same. Nevertheless, some behaviour patterns are more common than others. Getting out of the water is certainly most common when the baby's birth is imminent. But there are exceptions: even for a first baby and, more typically, for subsequent births, the end of the delivery can be very fast in the water.

Birth Under Water

It is important to know that birth under water is a possibility, though this is not necessarily the aim: in any birthing place where a pool is available, underwater birth is bound to happen every so often. Equally important is the knowledge that the new-born baby is perfectly adapted to immersion.

When a woman feels that her baby is going to be born in the water, and when she obviously does not want to be disturbed, it is useless and dangerous to insist on her getting out of the water, perhaps in a panic with the risk of a broken leg on a slippery floor.

Once more, the best way to learn is to observe the mother herself. It is as if, having lost her inhibitions to such a degree, the mother suddenly overcomes any fear of the water and reaches a state of consciousness in which she *knows* that there is no risk of the baby being drowned and that it can be born safely under water. She just lets the baby enter an environment that is familiar to him. A birth attendant (or the mother herself) has just to catch him at the bottom of the pool and bring him gently, in a matter of seconds but without rushing, to the surface. As soon as he is in a cool atmosphere, the baby starts to cry. Then the mother, who is often on her knees, is ready to hold the baby in her arms. The pool is sufficiently deep so that, if she is kneeling, the surface of the water is just below the breasts, making skin-to-skin contact and eye-to-eye contact as easy as possible.

Welcoming the baby in such an aquatic environment often evokes the expression of intense emotions without any restraint. Release of instincts, release of emotions . . . this is the heart of the matter. Later on, we will raise crucial questions about the nature and causes of inhibitions.

CHAPTER 2

Interpretations

How Water Works

There are simple explanations, accepted by everyone, as to how water actually works when the cervix is dilating.

Immersion in warm water tends to reduce the level of hormones that we secrete at a high rate when we are cold or frightened. It is well known that a high level of these hormones, which belong to the adrenalin family, makes the dilatation of the cervix take longer; it also becomes more difficult and more dangerous.

In addition, immersion in a small pool reduces the force of gravity. This has the effect of minimizing stimulation to that part of the inner ear called the vestibular system, which constantly gives information about the position and the orientation of the different parts of the body. When you add darkness and silence, sensory stimulation is reduced even further. When the woman lies back in the pool so that her ears are under the water, the outside world is cut off completely.

It is also possible that warm water acts directly on the muscular system. Tendons are composed mainly of collagen, and the warmer the temperature, the softer the collagen becomes. So a warm bath might have a direct relaxing effect.

Thus a bath that is the same temperature as the body protects the mother-to-be against the fight-and-flight response; it achieves the physiological state sometimes called 'relaxation response'.

Strangely enough, it is the process of getting *out* of the water, rather than the time spent *in* the water, that needs to be thought about and explained.

How Getting out of the Water Works

When the actual birth of the baby is not far off and contractions are no longer efficient while the woman is in the warm bath, how is it possible that suddenly going into a cooler atmosphere can trigger a speedy end to the labour? If you have a simplistic notion about the effects of adrenalin (and the other related hormones) on the birth process, then you are faced with a paradox. One is taught that cold, fear and generally all situations that go with a high level of adrenalin hinder the birth process. How, then, can this paradox be explained?

It is the phenomenon of the baby being born quickly once the woman has left the warm bath for the relative cool of the birthing room that prompted me to rehabilitate the phrase 'foetus ejection reflex'. This phrase was first introduced by the American scientist Dr Niles Newton in the 1960s, when she was studying the importance of environmental factors on the birth of mice. She discovered some efficient tricks to make the birth longer, more difficult and more dangerous: by putting the labouring animal in an unfamiliar place, where she could not smell or see what she was used to in her daily life; by moving the animal from place to place during the labour; or by reducing the sense of privacy by putting the animal in a transparent cage instead of an opaque one. Niles Newton suggested that the phrase 'foetus ejection reflex' might be a tool that can broaden our knowledge of the birth process, just as the phrase 'milk ejection reflex' can increase our understanding of the physiology of lactation.

I made the first step the day when I made a connection between the foetus ejection reflex set off by getting out of a warm bath and the same reflex set off by fear – a situation accompanied by a high level of adrenalin. I recalled, for example, that some old French doctors used to have the habit of saying something frightening before deciding to use forceps. When there were blacksmiths to shoe horses, these old doctors used to say things like '*Faîtes chauffer les fers!*' ('Heat up the iron tools!'), instead of simply asking to have the forceps ready. Now and again, this actually worked as a way of avoiding the need for forceps.

I also recalled some women overcome by a real phobia of

surgery, whose babies were lying in the breech position. Labour went well until complete dilatation of the cervix was reached and there it stopped. The time came when we had to decide to do a Caesarean and go to the operating theatre. The baby was born in the corridor on the way there.

From stories written by a traveller during the eighteenth century, I discovered that among the Iroquois Indians of Canada labouring women isolated themselves in a small hut and usually had quick and easy deliveries. However, if the labour was longer and more difficult than normal, the young people of the tribe were called and surprised the labouring woman by all shouting together. This was supposed to have done the trick, and the baby was born soon afterwards.

Even so, there are several authentic cases of the foetus ejection reflex that are not set off by either a sudden difference of temperature or by anything frightening. So what, I wanted to know, did all these births have in common?

In all the cases mentioned the period of dilatation of the cervix takes place in an atmosphere of complete privacy. For example, the mother-to-be is alone in her own bathroom or bedroom, while the baby's father is busy somewhere else. The woman knows that an experienced person is at hand. Also, she has not been disturbed by a vaginal exam. Suddenly, her voice and her whole demeanour change. A cry or a gesture means 'Help me, come quickly!' or something she says shows she is frightened. Often what she says has something to do with death. The main point is that a woman is free to express her fears without being restrained by reassuring words. Bouts of anger can also happen during a short period of time: I have known women to bang their elbows against the wall, or things like that. Once this stage is reached, if the woman is free to scream, it is the point of no return. Nothing can interrupt the foetus ejection reflex now – not even orders to push, orders not to push or to breathe like this, or breathe like that! During these very last contractions the woman has a sudden muscular strength of great magnitude, grasping either somebody or something.

This sudden burst of energy probably coincides with a high level of adrenalin. She will have a dry mouth and a sudden thirst for a glass of water. Her pupils are dilated. Looking back, some women remember a brief state of panic just before the onset of the storm, and that is how I came to the concept of physiological fear. In other words, at a certain stage of labour, the expression of some kind of fear can be considered normal. This is not specific to humans. Anxiety is the main emotion seemingly expressed by many mammals when giving birth. However, perhaps it is artificial to consider fear as the only emotion that precedes the foetus ejection reflex. There is such a mixture of emotions!

Any strong emotion is accompanied by *a reduction in neocortical control, which is the prerequisite for a fast and easy birth.* This means less control by the intellect. When rational control is reduced, one tends to forget what has been learned, what is cultural. During any kind of sexual experience all the inhibitions come from the neocortex, the part of the brain that is so strongly developed in humans. In order to understand the meaning of physiological fear, one has to get rid of the simplistic vision of the effects of fear and adrenalin. The injection of adrenalin during childbirth gives contradictory results. Often adrenalin can inhibit the process, but in certain circumstances it can speed it up. To summarize, one can say that during the first stage of labour adrenalin (and the other catecholamines) have an inhibiting effect. But after a certain stage is reached in the labour, they can set off the foetus ejection reflex.

To accept the concept of physiological fear, one must also forget any distinction between positive and negative emotions. This differentiation makes no sense to physiologists. All emotions have some role to play. In the wild, when a female animal is threatened by a predator at the start of her labour, the inhibition of labour is an advantage. The rush of adrenalin temporarily halts the birth process and makes it possible for the animal to fight or run away. On the other hand, at the end of labour, the opposite is the case. If the animal is under threat, it is best to deliver the offspring as quickly as possible, so a rapid foetus ejection reflex is a positive advantage.

Like physiological fear, physiological pain has a role to play during labour. It triggers the secretion of endorphins, which help the secretion of prolactin, the hormone needed for the production of milk. Prolactin is also the hormone that completes the maturation of the baby's lungs – a process that happens during childbirth. This example demonstrates the interconnectedness of all the physiological processes.

This new vision of the process of birth, inspired by the effects of getting out of water, underlines the artificiality of the conventional boundaries between the 'first stage' and the 'second stage' of labour. The real boundary is not the complete dilatation of the cervix. In an atmosphere of spontaneity – which is difficult to imagine when the extent of your horizons has been a conventional obstetric unit – the actual frontier is signposted by a change of behaviour, when the woman suddenly becomes active, violent, even aggressive. The foetus ejection reflex can begin before the dilatation of the cervix is complete. On the other hand, complete dilatation can precede this reflex.

Dilatation–Ejection . . . Erection–Ejaculation

This interpretation of the foetus ejection reflex suggests how complex, subtle, and therefore vulnerable is the normal process of childbirth in humans. Such an interpretation does not compete with other points of view or theories: the topic is new. Up to now, the priority has never been to improve our understanding of the normal processes. That is why for two decades the majority of Western babies have been born in an electronic environment without any proper evaluation of its effect on the physiological processes. Now all the reports published in the most authoritative medical journals agree that the only significant statistical effect of the electronic machine used during labour is to increase the rate of Caesareans and forceps deliveries.

This means that we are entering a new phase in the history of childbirth: let us call it the post-electronic era. Just because surgical teams in every hospital can safely perform this wonderful rescue operation called a Caesarean does not mean that we should stop trying to improve our understanding of the normal process of birth. The time has come to be more scientific.

In fact, our interpretation of the foetus ejection reflex has parallels with other episodes of the sexual life whose complexity has been studied in more detail, such as the ejaculation in male orgasm. Ejaculation is controlled by the sympathetic nervous system, which uses adrenalin – the hormone of aggression – as a mediator. The short phase of ejaculation is usually preceded by the longer phase of erection. This is under the control of the parasympathetic nervous system, which is inhibited by adrenalin. The physiological similarities between ejection and ejaculation are obvious.

By drawing this parallel between the foetus ejection reflex and ejaculation, the events of sexual life can be easily interpreted. They are a combination or a succession of passive episodes and active, violent, even aggressive ones.

The Baby's First Cry

We can learn a great deal from babies born under water. They give us a better understanding of birth as a passage from liquid into the air, and as an introduction to gravity.

It has been known for a long time that the foetus's lungs are filled with liquid, and the resistance to breathing in liquid is such that during an in-breath the liquid does not move more than one millimetre in the respiratory tract. It is only in very abnormal circumstances, such as a total deprivation of oxygen, that the liquid can be inhaled up to the pulmonary alveolus. But what is the main factor that triggers the first cry? Birth under water confirms that it is contact with the air.

Here are some anecdotes that underline the fact that air is all that is needed to stimulate the baby's first cry. I was attending the birth of a first baby. Its head was crowning when suddenly I heard the mysterious cry of a baby. Surprised by this unexpected event, I performed a large episiotomy, so that the baby could be born straight away. I found out afterwards that this young mother had previously had an operation on a fistula, that is an abnormal connection between the vagina and rectum. The fistula had opened during the delivery and, at the very moment when the baby's mouth came alongside the fistula, thus making contact with the air, the baby gave its first cry.

In Bogotá I met an obstetrician who told me an amazing story. During the 1950s he had tried to find out the details of a placenta by injecting oxygen into the uterus before taking an X-ray (this technique has since been abandoned). Immediately after injecting the oxygen, he heard a baby crying. The baby cried again, and he was able to make a recording of it. Three weeks later a healthy little girl was born – who had become an adult by the time I heard this story. This shows that contact with a gaseous environment was enough to trigger a cry without altering, in the weeks following, the baby's perfect adaptation to a liquid environment.

For a long time it has also been well known that cold is another triggering factor of the baby's first breath. Splashing the baby's chest with alcohol or ether, or going from a warm bath to a cold bath, have both been used in the past when the new-born baby did not cry straight away. Birth under water has helped us evaluate the importance of this factor.

I remember the story of a baby who was born under water in July on one of the hottest days anyone could remember in France. The steam from the water in the bath made the air even hotter. Once the baby had been taken out of the bath, we had to wait longer than usual for the first cry. However, even in very hot countries the difference in temperature between the water and the atmosphere is always sufficient; the baby is born wet, and so loses enough warmth in the first seconds.

While scientists are concerned about the factors that trigger the first cry, mothers wonder about its meaning. The first cry of a new-born baby might be the equivalent of the 'distress vocalizations' studied by the American scientist Jaak Panksepp. Panksepp reproduced such vocalizations by stimulating some very precise zones of the primitive brain of the guinea pig, which are rich in endorphins. These vocalizations follow the termination of brain stimulation and are similar to those that occur in addicted animals during opiate withdrawal. The first cry might correspond with a sudden change in the level of endorphins. For physiologists, the meaning of this 'panic behaviour' is a call for social cohesion. These experiments indicate the location in the primitive brain of the emotional command system that is attuned to social loss. The first cry may mean 'Help!'

Other Questions

How long should the baby be kept under water? As soon as the baby is born, he should be brought gently to the surface, without rushing. But there are those who want to keep the baby under water longer, believing this will reduce the baby's distress. This is a dangerous belief, because the placenta can detach very quickly. The umbilical cord may be pulsating, but this does not mean the baby is safe; a pulsating cord simply indicates the baby is still alive. To try to get rid of only the physiological distress of the new-born is like trying to get rid of only the pain during the labour, or only the fear, or only the screams. In the period around birth, one cannot eliminate what is just one link of a highly complex combination of physiological processes, without disturbing all of it. The usual way to alleviate the physiological distress of the new-born is to facilitate skin-to-skin contact between mother and baby as soon as possible.

New-born babies have survived under water for as long as forty minutes. An experiment made in France by Edwards as early as 1824 showed that new-born dogs can survive up to fifty-four minutes under water. It has also been shown that new-born rats can remain under water for forty minutes at body temperature and become normal adults, and even exist for up to eighteen hours in a salt-water solution equilibrated with oxygen at high pressure. New-born mammals have an enormous tolerance to lack of oxygen.

One must not forget the questions raised by obstetricians when they hear about the use of water during labour. Their main concern is the risk of infection. It is strange that doctors who do not hesitate to rupture membranes, repeatedly to carry out vaginal examinations and to insert catheters or electrodes are frightened by the idea that a labouring woman might have a bath. When I wrote an article on this topic in 1983 in a medical journal, I used discretion, claiming that the use of water during labour required further research, although at that time we had had no infection complications. Now that the use of water is a daily practice in places as far apart as Upland (California), Ostend (Belgium), Melbourne, Malta and Cornwall, it is obvious that fear of infection is not inspired by the facts.

When the mother-to-be enters the bath at the stage of hard labour, and when there is a good degree of dilatation of the cervix, she is not likely to stay in the water long enough to make the reproduction of germs possible. Also, the vagina is much more waterproof than is commonly thought (this has been shown by introducing vaginal tampons impregnated with chemicals that are able to react with a chemical introduced into the water). Dangerous germs are not in tap water. Mother and baby, who share the same antibodies, have a special resistance to germs that surround the mother's body. In London, where it is possible to rent a transportable pool for the period of birth, parents are given a thin plastic disposable liner, so that the fear of germs lurking from a previous birth is eliminated. And, finally, the use of water avoids some obstetric interventions such as forceps, vacuum extraction and Caesareans, which bring their own risk of infection.

Birth under water is also an opportunity to pose some questions about the different sensory functions of the new-born baby and his mother. One might wonder whether birth under water weakens the new-born baby's sense of smell. After a water-birth in a warm and humid atmosphere the mother and her baby do not smell the same as after ordinary birth. Doesn't water-birth interfere with the mother identifying her baby, and the baby identifying its mother? What is certain is that birth under water does not prevent an early sucking in the first half-hour following birth, although the sense of smell probably plays some part in this event.

When a baby is born under water, the parents become aware of their baby's perfect adaptation to an aquatic environment, and they ask themselves how this can be maintained. Other questions follow, such as how to develop the baby's capacity to adapt to weightlessness. The organ related to adaptation to gravity (the vestibular system in the inner ear) is very complex. One part of it (the utricle and saccule) is sensitive to linear accelerations such as those caused by gravity, while the other part (the semicircular canals) is sensitive to movements of the head in relation to the rest of the body. Because this organ matures when the child is very young, it means that any training for weightlessness, which would involve developing the ability to dissociate different functions of the vestibular system, must begin at an early age. Questions such as these might prove important for members of future generations, who will have to explore both space and the aquatic universe.

Childbirth at a Turning Point

When I am asked about the advantages of having a pool in a maternity hospital, I usually reply: 'It's a way to raise important questions.' Until the present time childbirth in our society has inspired two questions. The first one is: 'How can childbirth be controlled?' This is the foremost question for doctors. It is this that made women lie on their backs; it is this that concentrated births in huge hospitals; it is this that made electronic foetal monitoring the symbol of modern obstetrics. This question stops doctors from seeing that when you either observe or control an event of sexual life, you inhibit it.

The second question is: 'How can one help a woman giving birth?' This question leads to teaching women how they should give birth. Fernand Lamaze said that a woman must learn to give birth in the same way that one learns how to read, or to write, or to swim. In America, Robert Bradley thought that one could teach a woman and her husband the part each of them would play at the time of the birth. He thought that the husband might take on the role of coach. The problem with this is that understanding birth as an involuntary process becomes ever more remote. One simply cannot help an involuntary process; one can only disturb it.

When you analyse how a warm bath works – by protecting against too much sensory stimulation and anything that can set off a fight-and-flight response – a fundamental question is raised, one we must ask in the midst of the current obstetrical crisis, one we were trained to avoid at medical school: what can disturb the involuntary process of birth?

The answer is found in the non-human mammals. Giving birth is a solitary experience for mammals. When the birth is imminent, they isolate themselves. The pregnant sheep, normally a herd dweller, separates herself from her cohorts; the rat, normally a nocturnal prowler, gives birth during the day; and the horse, a daytime grazer, gives birth during the night. The priority of labouring females is not to avoid predators but to protect themselves from members of their own species.

The fundamental question is, why? Experiments that obliged the marmoset to give birth in full view with a light on showed the point at which the female was in trouble, and how the birth and first contact with the offspring were disturbed by the group's curiosity and intense need for activity. In our society, pregnant women and breast-feeding mothers, who need strong social support, are isolated. But labouring women at the time when they need privacy, are observed by several people as well as, sometimes, a machine. Interestingly enough, in cultures where the mother-to-be can isolate herself to give birth, childbirth has the reputation of being fast and easy. We have subtle and powerful ways to destroy the sense of privacy, and these are not particular to hospital births: establishing eye-to-eye contact when the mother-to-be is ready to 'go to another planet', as if saying, 'Stay with me'; performing an internal examination at the wrong time; introducing a camera . . .

A camera is much more dangerous than is commonly thought. There was a time when we found it useful to make some photos and TV programmes to change the mental pictures associated with the word 'birth'. But the camera was mentioned or introduced only at the point of no return, when the delivery could not be inhibited in any way. Now it is essential to stop the epidemic of videos and photos, as they commonly contribute to long and difficult births. But our society as a whole – and human cultures in general – cannot easily understand the need for the labouring woman's privacy.

Finally, these considerations about other mammals and the need for privacy suggest that immersion in a pool of water might provide the mother with an opportunity for isolation and eliminate useless stimulation, particularly the kind that can be found in the context of a hospital. This may also explain why a shower in a small private room can be more efficient than a bath in a large busy one. Another effect of an aquatic environment might be to calm nervous birth attendants and reduce their need for activity.

CHAPTER 3
The Power of Water

Consciousness-raising

A couple of anecdotes might help throw some light on the power of water. A young woman was in labour for several hours. The dilatation of the cervix seemed to have stopped. The contractions were strong, painful and frequent, but one had the feeling that they were getting her nowhere. This was the right time to mention the pool, and even to fill it. The young woman could hear the sound of the water. She looked with fascination at the nice blue water. The baby was then born on the floor, before the pool was filled.

What first led me towards an awareness of the magical properties of water was the incredible interest shown by journalists in birth under water. At first we were often irritated by reporters who came to our maternity unit and seemed interested in the babies born under water. We wanted to show them how we were doing everything we could to adapt the environment to the needs of mothers and babies, and to help mothers towards a better understanding of the process of birth and the start of the mother–baby relationship. But we were disappointed to find they were often not interested in these aspects. But there was something to be learned from this. Journalists usually have their fingers on the pulse of what interests the general public. They can predict how their audience (readers, viewers or listeners) will respond emotionally. They know, or rather they have an instinct, about what will capture the public's imagination. They feel that water has a power that cannot be fully expressed in the dry language of physiologists.

Few programmes on French television left a deeper impression than the series *The Baby is a Person*. From an analytical point of view, it was easy to criticize. At first the baby is the opposite of a person. The word 'person' means the image we give of ourselves in the society we belong to. Originally, 'persona' meant the mask an actor wears, and the part he plays. A new-born baby has no mask. It expresses feelings uncontrollably. The sequence that attracted most attention was a birth under water taken with an underwater camera. Serious people were indignant, including some from our own team. When you have only a few minutes to show the hospital at Pithiviers, isn't it a sacrilege to show nothing other than a birth under water? However, this programme was undoubtedly a great success. Defying in advance all the critics, the producers knew the power of a new-born baby and the power of water. They knew how to get an emotional response that could grab the viewers.

In Great Britain I often heard people talking about the BBC documentary *Birth Reborn* long after it had been screened. Some people remembered only the scenes of the birth under water, a sequence that comprised three minutes of a forty-minute programme.

A network of people from all over the world who are impassioned by birth under water has spontaneously appeared, and they have been instrumental in raising consciousness about the power of water. We shall call them the water-birth mafia.

The Water-birth Mafia

The members of this unofficial network believe that birth under water is a stage in the evolution of mankind. Many of them left their careers and started a new life devoted to a cause they felt must take priority over everything else. All of them are concerned by man's continuing destruction of the planet. Included in this network are mothers, women without children and men. Several became travellers drawn by two poles: Moscow and Pithiviers.

While at Pithiviers the starting point was to try to make labour easier and to avoid drugs, in Moscow it was underwater birth. Originally, Igor Tcharkovsky was a swimming instructor and taught physical education. From the beginning of the 1960s he focused his interest on the capacities of human babies in water. He realized that the younger the baby is, the better his adaptation to water. He learned a great deal from his own daughter, who was born prematurely and, as a new-born infant, spent the best part of her time in water. Instead of giving the baby a supplement of oxygen, which can have negative side effects, it can be wiser to reduce his need for oxygen; one way to do this is by entering the water and eliminating gravity. This is how Tcharkovsky became involved in birth under water.

Tcharkovsky also has a special interest in the relationship between humans and dolphins, and particularly between dolphins and pregnant women and babies. He observed that children can establish contact with dolphins immediately, without any preliminary preparation, as if they had known each other for a long time. New-born babies make this contact with most ease, and adults can not apprehend it. Tcharkovsky thinks that the presence of the dolphin instantaneously and naturally relieves the baby and his mother of the fear of water, even at night. Tcharkovsky remembers instances when dolphins politely interfered when he was training a child and took the infant out over the surface of the water. Probably the little one was not feeling quite well, and the dolphin received the signal for help that we cannot understand. Magazines in several Western countries have recorded births that were assisted by a dolphin midwife.

Tcharkovsky is also interested in extrasensory perception – ways of communicating that cannot be explained by scientific methods in the Western world. He believes that being born under water and cultivating adaptation to water are ways of developing the powers of telepathy and clairvoyance. In a country where the religious instinct is denied, he asks about man's spiritual dimension and its development.

Many different roads lead to the water-birth mafia. There are mothers who gave birth under water. There are people who are mostly interested in man's adaptation to an aquatic environment. Such is the case of Jacques Mayol, author of *Homo delphinus*, the diver who can go down more than a hundred metres without oxygen. Mayol visited Tcharkovsky in Moscow and brought a Japanese TV crew to Pithiviers as part of a programme about men and water. For others, the starting point is an interest in dolphins. Some in the water-birth mafia are therapists who practise rebirthing. ('States of regression' or 'changes of conscious levels' are triggered by different kinds of conscious breathing. The process is seen as a way to activate zones of the primitive part of the brain, upon which are imprinted previous experiences such as the birth itself.) Others are journalists, writers or producers whose lives changed after being in touch with the water-birth mafia. Yet others are midwives who have not shrunk from assisting births under water at home, in Europe, the USA, New Zealand, Australia or South Africa. Even some doctors belong to the mafia.

Many people are aware of the power of water during childbirth without becoming obsessed with birth under water to the point of claiming that it will save humanity. How they reach this awareness can, again, be very varied. Janet Balaskas, who runs the Active Birth Centre in London, told me this story. At the end of a long yoga session, before the pregnant women recovered their normal state of consciousness, she asked them: 'Where would you most like to give birth?' 'Water, or somewhere with water in it,' were common replies. In general, women dream of giving birth in a natural environment. No one dreams of a hospital or even of a bedroom. It is worth remembering that Freud interpreted dreams of water as being about birth.

The Tcharkovsky Phenomenon

I cannot help seeing connections between what I call the Leboyer Phenomenon, the profound effects of a succession of his works of art on the general public and the Tcharkovsky Phenomenon.

In both cases there is water and there are new-born babies. Of all Leboyer's numerous works, a lot of people remember only that in his book *Birth without Violence* and his first film, he gave a bath to a new-born baby. Nobody knows better than Leboyer that, above all else, the new-born needs his mother's arms. But it was the artist Leboyer who gave the baby a bath. Interestingly enough, Leboyer – the artist of this century who will have the greatest influence on the health and way of life of the next generations – introduced water into all his books and films.

In the book *Loving Hands* the infant is given a bath after a massage by Shantala. At the end of the film *Loving Hands* we are on a beach watching and hearing the waves. In the book *Le Sacre de la naissance* the stage of labour that precedes the last contractions is symbolized by the anger of the ocean, which, instead of intimidating, stimulates. The words are reinforced by the famous painting of Hokusai, *Waves of Kanagawa*. In the silent film *Breathing* the emotions of the labouring woman are expressed through the sight and the sound of water.

The work of Tcharkovsky has points in common with the work of Leboyer in so far as it is guided primarily by intuition, faith, beliefs, feelings, clairvoyance; it is bound up with the unknown, mystery, perhaps even legend. And like Leboyer, Tcharkovsky does not communicate his knowledge via medical or scientific literature. He will have an indirect influence on our understanding of the human phenomenon but apparently most people associate him only with birth under water and birth among dolphins.

The Tcharkovsky phenomenon cannot be dissociated from the need for legends all human societies have, especially legends about aquatic human beings.

Water as a Symbol

Where does the extraordinary power of water come from? Niko Saito, a Japanese teacher who is passionate about the adaptation of babies to water, gave me a simple answer on a postcard after she had visited Pithiviers: 'For man, water represents a mother's affection.' This is not exclusive to either Japanese or Western cultures. Water has always been the symbol of the mother everywhere and at all times. Life began in the ocean; in amniotic fluid we recapture the history of life. The attraction of water during labour and dreams of aquatic births are not new.

In ancient Greece, Aphrodite, the goddess of love, was born from the foam of the waves. In Cyprus the goddess of love was born on the beach at Paphos. According to a Japanese tradition, women living in some small villages by the sea gave birth in the sea. Engravings suggest that in some African tribes the traditional place to give birth was near a river. Some aborigines on the western coast of Australia first paddle in the sea and then give birth on the beach. Birth under water was probably known in cultures as diverse as the Indians of Panama and, perhaps, some Maoris of New Zealand.

But it is mainly in the realms of dream, fantasy and metaphor that birth and water are commonly associated. Aquatic metaphors can be adapted to the different phases of labour: the first stage does not conjure up the same images of water as the ejection of the foetus, the phase of violent, aggressive and even frightening waves. In fact, all episodes of sexual life have been expressed in water metaphors – from the romantic lake to the rhythmic waves of orgasm . . .

CHAPTER 4

The Erotic Power of Water

Poets and Legends

Seas, oceans, lakes, ponds, springs, wells, streams, waves, rivers, clouds, rain, fountains ... water has always been a powerful inspiration for the imagination. When you realize how important fantasies are in sexual life, it is clear that there is a close relationship between Eros and water. This relationship has always inspired poets, no matter which language they speak.

> *Dans la cour le jet d'eau qui jase*
> *Et ne se tait ni nuit ni jour,*
> *Entretient doucement l'extase*
> *Où ce soir m'a plongé l'amour*

> – Charles Baudelaire, '*Le Jet d'eau*'

> Blonde Aphrodite rose up excited
> Moved to delight by the melody,
> White as an orchid she rode quite naked
> In an Oyster shell on top of the sea

> W. H. Auden,
> 'Song for St Cecilia's Day'

In every land, in every age, myths, tales and legends have testified to the irresistible erotic power of water. In Greek mythology the hunter Actaeon unintentionally surprised the goddess Artemis bathing naked in the woods. Artemis – whose name is associated with chaste love – protected herself by changing Actaeon into a stag, so that his dogs killed him. In the Bible, King David caught Bathsheba unaware while she was taking a bath, and this fired him with violent desire.

The legends about mermaids are mysterious because they are universal. There is always an erotic and romantic aura surrounding them. The mermaid represents the *femme fatale* of the sea. Regardless of the era, the place or the climate, all legends about mermaids are variations of the same theme.

The typical mermaid has the head and body of a woman. Her hair is long and beautiful, her beauty and charm irresistible. But below the waist the mermaid is like a fish, with scales and fins. Usually the mermaid falls in love with a human man, marries him and shares his life for a short time, until the day when something or other breaks their contract, and she goes back to her true home in the sea, or sometimes a lake, a river, or even the water in a well. In some legends, it is the man who temporarily shares aquatic life with a mermaid, or else it is the male who is half man and half fish. There is even a legend about a couple who were half human and half fish who lived in the Nile Delta.

Mermaids can be found in a multitude of English and Scottish legends. One of the best known is the Cornish mermaid whose likeness adorns a pew-end in the fifteenth-century church at Zennor, in which, according to tradition, she often sat. A mermaid is supposed to be responsible for the fact that Padstow Harbour is now so choked with sand that it cannot take the large ships any more. A man shot at this mermaid one day as she was disporting herself in the sea, and, before disappearing, she vowed that the harbour should be for ever desolate . . . There is some hope that the parsons might find a way out of the mermaid's curse. It is also in Cornwall that several families are supposed to possess mysterious powers as a legacy of their mermaid ancestry. As for the Scottish mermaids and their kin, they outnumber all the others in the British Isles. There are countless love-affairs between Scottish mermaids and mortals. A shepherd and a mermaid fell in love, but after a time the young man came no more to the rocky shore that had been their trysting place. Her heart broken, the mermaid dashed herself to pieces against the entrance of the arch of a cave that she had haunted in the days of her happiness. It is said that the arch kept the clear impression, in dull red, of the mermaid's form.

The British mermaids have their European equivalents: Melusina from the French Middle Ages; Merrimini or Meerfrun from German legends; Mermennill from Ireland; Mari Morgan from Brittany; Morfowyn from Wales; or the Russian Rusalka. These also have a lot in common with the Japanese Mujina, the Chinese mermaid who bathes in a well, the African and American Indian mermaids, and the fish-tailed divinities that appear in early Greek vase paintings.

Scientists who are not aware of the importance of fantasies in eroticism, particularly in the erotic life of sailors, or of the power of water on man's imagination, have had to construct simplistic theories to explain the legends about mermaids. Some naturalists have claimed that there is nothing more to it than mistaking sea mammals who rise from the water to suckle their young for mermaids. No matter what mistakes might have been behind these legends, there is no doubt that the mysterious 'princesses of the water' can throw much light on humans and their relationship with water. The kingdom of water can raise us up, or let us sink into love and dreams.

Some Latin languages, including the French, have no specific word for mermaid. The French word *sirène* encompasses the concept, but to the ancient Greeks the siren was not a mermaid: she was a 'bird-woman' with the head and bust of a woman and the body and claws of a bird. It was Homer who gave the siren a glorious voice and turned her into the *femme fatale* of the sea – the emblem of feminine seduction that the world has accepted ever since. Unfortunately the sirens are only voices in the *Odyssey*. When he endowed them with voices of surpassing beauty, Homer did not tell us about the form of their bodies.

How did the metamorphosis from siren to mermaid come about? Nobody knows. There are many examples of transitional sirens, such as the one described in the bestiary of Guillaume Le Clerc:

24

Of the syren we shall tell you,
Which has a very strange form.
For from the waist upwards
She is the most beautiful thing in the world
Fashioned in the form of a woman.
The other part is shaped
Like a fish or like a bird . . .

The time came when siren and mermaid were one. When a medieval craftsman wished to carve a siren to symbolize the Lures of the Flesh, he almost invariably represented her as a fish-tailed mermaid.

While poets and legends have always expressed the erotic power of water, the fact is that no one knows exactly what this erotic power of water is. It has never been studied, not even by those who were interested in the symbolism of water, such as Gaston Bachelard in his study of water and dreams, or more recently Ivan Illich in H_2O *and the Waters of Forgetfulness*. In a masterly manner Illich demonstrates how, in industrialized societies in the era of sewers and bathrooms, water has been reduced to a utilitarian substance that can destroy the water of dreams. He makes a distinction between cleansing water and purifying water, between water as a domestic necessity and water as a religious and spiritual force. But, as he has done before, Illich declines to meet Eros. Whatever the topic, Illich masters the art of avoiding sexuality. In *Medical Nemesis* he sought to condemn the expropriation of health by exploring the various supposed aims of the medical professions: the suppression of pain, the eradication of disease and the struggle against death. But he never mentioned the control of fertility, pregnancy, childbirth, breast-feeding . . . Even in *Gender* he found a way to shun difficulties thanks to a subtle opposition between economic sex and vernacular gender. So his faithful readers were hardly expecting an allusion to the erotic power of water, even in a study entitled *The Water of Dreams*.

Dr Sandor Ferenczi, the disciple and friend of Freud, proposed an interpretation of the sexual act that gives an answer to this simple question: why is water, a feminine symbol, an erotic symbol for both men and women? In *Thalassa*, a study of the origins of sexual life, he considered the sexual act as a regression to the prenatal period, to life in the amniotic fluid. In other words, the sexual partner, male or female, is a kind of substitute for the mother. Modern neurophysiologists can understand this interpretation. A regression is what happens when the primitive brain is more or less liberated from the control of the neocortex. And this primitive brain, this old brain, reached its maturity early in life, mostly during the foetal period, in a liquid and feminine environment.

Taking Advantage of the Erotic Power of Water

Even though it may not be recognized or mentioned as such, the erotic power of water is constantly being used and even exploited.

Where do a young couple dream of when they plan a honeymoon? In Europe, they dream of Venice, with its endless canals, bridges and gondolas. In America, they dream of the Niagara Falls or Hawaii. In Niccolò di Segna's twelfth-century wedding scene (plate 5), taking place in the small Italian town of Siena, there is no sea, no lake, no river – but by tradition they knew how to use the erotic power of water.

Let us travel through space and time, in any direction, and we will find that people have always used the erotic power of water. In modern Japan, outside the hustle and bustle of the big cities, near the hills of Chichibu, they started a meeting place for teenagers called 'O-Miai Furo', which means 'dating in the tub'. After taking their clothes off, the boys and girls get into the open-air pool. The entrance for the girls is at one end of the pool, the one for the boys at the other. In the middle of the pool there is a movable screen above water level and a fixed barrier underneath it. When the screen is opened, the action starts. The management tosses a few oranges and lemons into the hot water and provides a floating card-table. Otherwise the teenagers are left to their own devices. According to the people who run this place, the boys and girls are more interested in talking to each other than in sex. However, this is a good example of genuine erotic art. Sexual interest is awakened by mystery, and fantasies are released with the help of water.

Water, Eroticism and Advertising

All over the world advertising agencies take advantage of the erotic power of water. Japanese women's magazines are a good example of this, particularly where cosmetics are concerned. One product claims to be 'the most sensuous natural moisturizer' and will 'leave your skin as soft as the shadow of a waterfall on a silken screen'. A colour advertisement shows a gorgeous young woman sitting up to her waist in a hot tub, voluptuously caressing her shoulder with a sponge; it is reminiscent of a mermaid. The product they are trying to make you buy may have nothing directly to do with water. It doesn't matter. They know that water in the ad will help sell it. For example, a well-known brand of Japanese films grabs your attention with pictures of attractive young women sunbathing. In the corner of the picture there is a hint of a blue pool.

Many advertising companies in the West are also masters in the art of using water to sell products. The Club Méditerranée stands out in this field. For several decades most of its ads have used water in some erotic way. I can think of one in particular aimed at the British public. A young woman, whose beautiful legs are still mysterious even though the wind is lifting her skirt, is walking upon the waves of the sea. She catches sight of a young man on a sailboat in a very suggestive position. The dialogue runs: 'I say, isn't that the good-looking limbo dancer from last night?' Many holiday companies and airlines all over the world have followed Club Méd's example.

Associating water with erotic meaning is one of the most common tricks used by advertising agencies to capture our attention. This mixture of water and eroticism is used for the most unlikely things: a temporary clerical staff agency, cigarettes, crispbread, after-shave lotion . . . Even pharmaceutical firms don't shrink from using sex and water to publicize drugs in professional medical magazines. To promote a drug that is supposed to lower blood pressure, they show the romantic scene of a couple rowing slowly on a quiet lake.

I have learned a great deal from chatting to people who work in advertising. They don't use the erotic power of water consciously.

But an artist does not need to be conscious of this potent force in order to use it. (By analysing this power, my approach is the opposite of the artist's.) A work of art communicates directly with the instinctive, emotional part of the brain in many individuals.

Eroticism and Painting

Great artists of the past have also used the symbol of water in their paintings to help induce erotic feelings. Even in the Middle Ages, Eros was present in some biblical scenes, for example when the beautiful Susannah is taking a bath, and a group of elders leer at her. The story of Susannah, as it is told in the Apocrypha, is a model of the erotic tale.

During the Renaissance, the relationship between man and nature was changing. Works such as *Perseus and Andromeda* by Titian or *Galatea* by Raphael transmit those things that are violent, aggressive and animalistic in eroticism, while the *Judgement of Paris* by Cranach expresses the part curiosity plays in eroticism. If you take away the water from these paintings, they don't attract your attention in the same way.

During the eighteenth century in France, Boucher knew that water was an integral part of an erotic atmosphere and not simply a setting. An example of this is his painting *The Setting of the Sun* (plate 7), in which Apollo meets Thetis, one of the fifty daughters of Nereus, God of the sea.

I wondered what we can learn about water from the Symbolists, those painters of the end of the nineteenth century whose declared ambition was to express emotions through symbols. I had a quick look at some of their paintings and selected those which, at first glance, had an erotic feel about them. I tried to analyse what these paintings had in common. They all had water in them. For example, in the works of Pierre Puvis de Chavannes the most suggestive paintings are *Girls by the Seashore*, with half-naked girls by the sea, and *The Dream*, with angels above the sea and women on the beach. Two paintings by Maurice Chabas can be called erotic: *Rêverie* and *Paysage*. The first one includes a landscape with mountains and lake and a young woman. The second one has both the mountains and the sea, a sea that is evaporating.

If you look at *The Shepherd's Song* by Puvis de Chavannes, and if you try and analyse the origin of its erotic force, you risk seeing nothing except three women expressing their receptivity, as if opening themselves to receive the shepherd's song . . . but there, in the background, is the sea . . .

Pictures of bodies that are half human and half snake inter-twined were done by Carlos Schwabe to illustrate some poems by Baudelaire. They are erotic in themselves . . . but this is heightened by placing them among waves. In *Satan's Treasure* by J. Delville you notice Satan, and snakes, and the intertwined bodies of naked men and women . . . But there is also, of course, water.

By the end of the nineteenth century the Symbolists did not have a monopoly on water as a symbol. There is also some water in *Narcisse* by Georges Desvallières, in *Luxe, calme et volupté* by Henri Matisse, in *Dawn of Love* by Charles Maurin, in *The Garden of Paradise* by Constant Montald. The most commercial painter of that time was Renoir, and he used to say that a painting was worth what people would pay for it. It is significant that Renoir knew very well the effects of water in a painting. One of his most highly regarded paintings is *La Femme au bain*.

The epoch of the Symbolists, the epoch of Renoir, was also the beginning of the period of Decadence. *L'art, les caresses et le Sphinx* by Fernand Knopff is the most representative painting of the Decadent period, and at the same time a perfect piece of erotic art. The sensuality and the tenderness expressed by the woman's face, the caress given by a hand linked with an animal's foreleg, the placing of the caress at the waist on the body of a half-naked young man, the direction the fingers are moving – all these put the work in the category of the most explicit eroticism. Even so, the water is there in the background, thus going beyond genitalia plain and simple!

It would take volumes to do an exhaustive study of the use of water as an erotic symbol in painting at the beginning of this century. However, certain works deserve to be singled out, such as Edvard Munch's *Lovers on the Shore*, *Young Girl on a Shore*, *Youth Bathing*, *Lovers in the Waves* and *Sunbathing*. A painting that exudes eroticism is *The Big Fish*, which brings together the three symbols characteristic of truly erotic scenes: a naked human body, an animal and water. It is not very far removed from the universal myths of the woman-fish and the man-fish. On a beach, close to the water, a big fish with masculine eyes and an erect tail seems to court a young naked woman with long hair. One could re-examine the entire history of painting from a new angle, focusing on the power of water. What would the smile of the Mona Lisa have been like if Leonardo da Vinci hadn't felt the power of water?

Other Forms of Art

Many sculptures were inspired by mermaids, not just the famous one in Copenhagen. Films too have made sex and water into a new art form. Before explicit sex was permissible, it was common to cut from 'couple kissing' to 'waves crashing on shore'. Can you imagine *La Dolce Vita* without the encounters in the fountain and the final scene on the beach? Why was the film *Castaway* so popular? It was based on the true story of a young woman who answered an ad in a magazine: 'Writer seeks wife for a year on a tropical island'. Legends about mermaids inspired the film *Miranda* and the play of the same name. Millions of viewers saw *Splash*. It is the age-old legend of the mermaid placed in the context of modern-day America. When the real identity of Madison, the mermaid of New York, is revealed by a zoologist, the first question the journalists ask her (human) boyfriend is: 'Did you make love in the water?' The success of such a film is enough to convince one that you cannot dissociate legends of mermaids from human nature. It helps us understand what is universal and transcultural among mankind.

The mermaid comes up again and again in music. In the catalogue of modern music in the British Library the list of works associated with the key word 'mermaid' takes up half-a-dozen pages. Mermaids play a central role in several operas. The Russian nymph, the *rusalka*, gave her name to an opera.

Johann Strauss's waltz has a title that makes you dream of lovely blue water, even though the Danube is grey, dirty and muddy at Vienna. 'The Blue Danube' became the most famous waltz in the world. And well-known popular singers such as

Maurice Chevalier knew the trick of arousing erotic feelings: 'Ça c'est passé un dimanche, un dimanche au bord de l'eau.'

Common Knowledge

Many restaurant owners know how to create the right atmosphere and to put people in a relaxed mood. They site their restaurants near a river, a lake or the sea, or else place an aquarium, a fountain, a painting of a raging sea or a still lake in the dining-room.

Thousands of lovers know how exciting a gentle massage with soapy water can be in the bath or under the shower. Making love in the bathroom is more common than one thinks. Making love in a tropical sea is much more than a fantasy, as is making love on a riverbank or on the beach. And why are water-beds so popular?

In his famous novel *The Comedians* Graham Greene tells the story of a young woman gripping the ledge of a swimming-pool so she can be approached from the rear by a man swimming with her. Now that diving is a popular sport, opportunities for underwater encounters between the sexes (such as in the James Bond movie *Thunderball*) have multiplied.

Pornographic Art

While the power of water is common knowledge and has been used since time immemorial by artists, it is nevertheless paradoxical that water is used hardly at all in pornographic art. Whether you consider drawing, painting, sculpture, film or novels, when the genital organs are revealed, water is no longer employed as a symbol. Maybe in this case it is no longer art. Maybe it is not eroticism either. Eros thrives on mystery, on symbols. True erotic art is not explicit but suggestive. It is also paradoxical that none of the well-known researchers in human sexuality have expressed any great interest in the use of water in sexual arousal.

Researchers in Human Sexuality

Henry Havelock Ellis, arguably the first modern sexologist, did not really raise the subject of water in his scholarly tomes published during the first three decades of this century. Even Ferenczi did not really study the erotic power of water; he confined himself to studying the origins of sexual life. He considered the sexual act as regression to the prenatal period, to life in amniotic fluid.

The Dutch gynaecologist Theodor Hendrik Van de Velde taught a whole generation of couples the art of copulation in his book *Ideal Marriage*, which was translated into several languages and ran to many editions. He taught the art of kissing and caressing. In a country that has such a special relationship with the sea, you might expect him to have given some space in his book to water.

Alfred Kinsey, who introduced the statistical method into the study of sexual behaviour, used to meet with artists and was interested in many forms of art. His death put an end to his study of eroticism in art. Perhaps he was on the verge of being aware of the power of water.

The famous *Hite Report*, which studies the sexual behaviour of American women, was based on very long questionnaires. There was not one question about the environment during sexual intercourse!

Sex Therapy

Perhaps it is even more surprising to find no reference to water in the advice given by the modern masters of sex therapy, William Masters and Virginia Johnson, and their disciples, neither in the different techniques of stimulation nor in the use of surrogates.

It is significant that the most authoritative books, such as *Human Sexual Response* and *Human Sexual Inadequacy* by Masters and Johnson or *The New Sex Therapy* by Helen Kaplan, fail to discuss the importance of the environment in general. The indifference of the sex therapists to environmental factors is comparable with the attitude of conventional obstetricians. Only an incredible lack of understanding about the needs of a woman in labour could have brought about a concentration of births in bigger and bigger obstetrical departments, with no effort made to make home births a real choice for women.

Even Glenn Wilson, a sex therapist who wrote a study about the sexual fantasies of men and women, was not interested in water. However, in his assessment of the fifteen most powerful fantasies, he found that making love in a romantic place such as a beach at night came second only to making love with a loved partner.

I became aware of these paradoxes after having to improvise the role of sex therapist on a few occasions. But my experience in this field is too limited to go beyond a couple of anecdotes.

One day I had a phone call from a young woman who wanted to have an appointment and to come along with her husband. In the space of one short telephone conversation she let me know she was infertile, adding that the main problem was her husband's virtual impotence. I suggested that the couple should visit me the following Sunday, at a time when we would not have to watch the clock. On the day the young woman arrived on her own, as her husband had given up the idea of coming. I saw her in the maternity department, thinking that a place full of mothers and babies could have only a positive effect on her. And, as she seemed to show an interest in the maternity unit itself, we did a tour of the birthing rooms, including the pool at the exact time when it was being filled with the lovely blue water. This is the place where we started chatting.

I understood that she had problems with ovulation, as she had only one or two periods a year. She also told me that her husband was going through a phase of having no sexual interest in her. Quite spontaneously, it occurred to me that the couple should come to the pool, either in the water or next to it, one night when nothing was happening in the maternity unit, so they could have complete privacy. This left the woman with plenty to dream about.

Some days later she called me and said that she and her husband found the suggestion appealing, but since they had talked to each other about being together in the water, their sexual activity had suddenly taken an upturn. Some weeks later she called me again and said she had a period. Some months later she was pregnant. The following year she came back to the maternity unit to give birth to her baby.

In a similar way, there were other times when I suggested to young couples having sexual difficulties that they should spend a few weeks together on a quiet beach. If I had read the works of the masters of sex therapy, my approach might have been quite different. Why should there be such a lack of attention to water in sex therapy, when the therapeutic power of water has been acknowledged for ages? Sex therapy concerns itself with technicalities, without going into much depth. So perhaps sex therapy is not a true therapy, just as pornographic art is not really art.

CHAPTER 5
The Tao of Medicine

When you're ill, you need a mother. Water is a feminine symbol. Water is the symbol of mother. In her book *Woman's Experience of Sex*, Sheila Kitzinger shows a picture of two children having a bath with their mother as a typical secure and loving scene. Is it surprising that throughout the world water has always been associated with the art of healing?

I remember chatting with a friend of mine, a doctor who was an adviser to the French national health insurance. He deplored the fact that many French doctors prescribe treatments in thermal spas just to please their patients. He tried to assess the cost to the French social security system of all these prescriptions. In countries like France, Austria, West Germany, Switzerland, Yugoslavia and the Soviet Union the health services reflect public opinion on this and officially recognize the benefit of spas. In spite of this, most doctors don't take spas very seriously. This friend was one of them, and he was sure most of his colleagues shared his point of view and prescribed spas only 'just to please' people. Here again water presents us with a universal, trans-cultural phenomenon. Throughout the ages and in all parts of the globe people have known and used the therapeutic power of water. Only a modern medical training can obliterate a knowledge so deeply imprinted in human beings. Interestingly enough, the most demonstrative studies evaluating the efficiency of spas have been carried out by insurance companies, notably the French Caisse Nationale d'Assurance Maladie.

Spas

One has to ask why such a widespread phenomenon as the spa has not inspired more reflection. Legend has it that in Japan a white heron led the first visitor, a wandering god, to the famous Takaragawa hot springs. Traditional Chinese medical practitioners knew how to use hot and cold springs. The American Indians knew about the healing properties of the hot springs in Arkansas. In ancient Greece the healing temples dedicated to Aesculapius, the god of medicine, were usually built near springs known for their healing powers.

Most of the European watering places were in use at the time of the Romans. Bath, the famous spa town in south-west England, was then known as Aquae Sulis, which means the 'waters of the goddess Sul'.

In the Middle Ages, the Church fathers tolerated the baths on the condition that they were used only for health and cleanliness purposes. These conditions are significant: they hint at the erotic connotations of the baths. One can guess that baths were also places to meet people. This is a reminder of how artificial it is to separate the therapeutic and the erotic powers of water.

During the eighteenth century the Belgian town of Spa became the most fashionable watering place in Europe. Since then the word 'spa' has become synonymous with curative waters.

With the enormous advances in pharmacology and modern surgery, some doctors predicted the decline, even the disappearance of spas. In fact, the opposite has happened. Yet again, water presents us with some contradictions. While on the one hand orthodox medical practitioners remain ignorant of the power of water and do not possess the means to comprehend the amplitude of the phenomenon, on the other hand spas have developed to an unprecedented extent throughout the world. Aix-les-Bains, Bains-les-Bains, Chateauneuf-les-Bains, Digne-les-Bains, Evian-les-Bains, Fumades-les-Bains, Gréoux-les-Bains – all these French towns, proud of their 'baths', derive a large part of their revenue from the therapeutic use of their curative waters. One could also mention all those towns whose names end in *les thermes* or that include the words *eaux* or *aigues*. Then there are also famous places associated with water but without explicit names, such as Vichy, Vittel, Royat, La Bourboule and Bagnoles de l'Orne.

In Germany there are countless towns whose names start with *Bad*. There must be more than 150 spas in Germany, and about six million people visit them each year. Very often the price of the cure is covered by the health system, which allows the long tradition of water therapies in the German-speaking countries to continue. In the nineteenth century the Austrian Vincenz Priessnitz, 'the Devil of Grafenberg', made the sitz-baths popular. The patient sits in a hot bath up to the waist, and then in a cold bath. There must still be scores of spas in Germany that follow the principles of Father Kneipp, an enthusiastic disciple of Priessnitz.

In modern industrial Japan you can hear people talk about the 'onsen boom' created by a TV travel show. 'Onsens' are the hot springs, and there are about 2,000 of them in Japan offering all kinds of cures to the Japanese people, and some also to their animals.

In the United States there are more than 300 hotels, motels and boarding houses at Hot Springs National Park alone, which together can accommodate more than a million visitors every year.

The development of hot springs along the Dead Sea has gone hand in hand with the rapid increase of health centres and hotels. The magic properties of the Dead Sea, which in Israel is called Yam Hamelach – 'the sea of salt' – have been known for a long time. Certainly the Dead Sea cannot be compared with any other stretch of water. It is a large salt lake 400 metres below sea level, a real sun trap with very high evaporation. As a result its water contains seven times more salt than that of the ocean. The Dead Sea resorts have a reputation for the successful treatment of psoriasis and rheumatism. The Roman historian Flavius was aware that travellers brought salt back from the Dead Sea because of its therapeutic virtues. Nowadays salt crystals from the Black Sea are commercialized for the same reasons.

The efforts of modern medicine to attempt to establish the theoretical basis of the effects of spas cannot match the amplitude of the phenomenon. Those who attempt to introduce a semblance of rationality into our understanding of how spas work are usually concerned only with things like the composition of the mineral salts or gas, the temperature, the radioactivity or some other physical properties such as density and quantity of mud. All these chemical or physical properties depend upon the origin of the water. Every sort of water has its own history. Some originates deep in the earth and comes welling up to the surface in chimneys. It can be hot, radioactive, and may contain rare gases. The hot springs, the geysers, belong to this group. Other water originates deep in the earth but has welled up close to the surface. Other water, having infiltrated the soil, remains superficial.

Depending on the differences in the composition of the mineral salts, the waters of some spas have a good reputation for the treatment of obesity; others for the treatment of digestive diseases; cardiovascular diseases; skin diseases; lung diseases; kidney diseases; etc. However, the rare scientific studies of the physiological effects of baths suggest that the mineral content is not very important. A well-known medical journal published an investigation into the clinical effects of immersion in the waters of Bath. After having drunk 400 ml of the local mineral water, the patients spent two hours in the water, at a temperature of 35°C. Blood and urine samples were taken and analysed, and variation in weight, amount of urine and blood dilution were also assessed. This kind of treatment can have huge measurable biological effects. But there was absolutely no difference between the effects of the water from Bath and that of ordinary tap water.

It is also usual for doctors to attribute the benefits of spas to a temporary change in the environment, to a change in lifestyle, and to being away from one's daily worries. *But they never talk about the water itself* or about the powerful impact of symbols on our emotional state, and therefore on our health.

Thalassotherapy

Spas have maintained their allure and their reputation. But in the last thirty years or so other forms of water therapy have developed as well. One such is thalassotherapy, in which the sea is used for therapeutic ends. Certainly there is nothing new in this. Four centuries before Christ, Euripides claimed that the sea could cure all human diseases. In the eighteenth century the English doctor Richard Russell praised the healing properties of sea water. In the nineteenth century, in France, an old nanny knew that the best way to cure children with rickets was to bathe them in the sea at Berck-Plage, which became the first sun-and-sea centre.

The first thalassotherapy centre was created at Roscoff in Britanny by Dr René Bagot, who followed the teachings of his father. Thalassotherapy always makes me think of the story of a young man whose leg was broken in a car accident. While he was in hospital, all he could think about was the time when he would be able to start his rehabilitation in a thalassotherapy centre. The word 'thalassotherapy' has also been popularized by the champion cyclist Louison Bobet, who was the sponsor and driving force behind one of these centres.

Thalassotherapy incorporates baths of different temperatures, massage, underwater exercises, pressurized jets of water, seaweed packs and even vaginal irrigation. To rationalize the effects of thalassotherapy, a similarity usually is drawn between the minerals and trace elements in sea water and in blood and extracellular fluids. The process of osmosis is often mentioned, whereby minerals and trace elements are absorbed through the skin, especially when the water has been heated to the same temperature as the body.

A real 'home thalassotherapy' – the absorption or injection of Quinton plasma – has been used extensively in France for half a century, particularly for dehydrated babies. Quinton plasma is no more or less than sea water sold in ampules. This therapy was based originally on the famous interpretations of Claude Bernard, who understood how the sea is deep inside all of us, and introduced the concept of the *milieu intérieur*. It is as if, little by little during the process of evolution, living creatures have transformed the primordial sea of nutrients into sap, lymph or blood. This interpretation was reinforced by the experiments of René Quinton. After taking 425 g of blood from a 10 kg dog, Quinton then induced a deep coma in the animal. Then the blood was replaced by diluted sea water. The dog recovered very quickly. Sea water has also been packaged in nebulizers to treat sinusitis.

Other Water Therapies

It is impossible to review all the possible ways of using water in therapy. In any era water has always played an important role in therapy in one form or another. Baths and wet packs have been used by some psychiatrists and psychotherapists. Some therapies use immersion in water to induce and exploit deep states of regression. 'Rebirthers' fully understand this power of water; they claim that a deep regression is more easily induced with the help of water.

In France, the medium of water is used to help autistic children become socialized. It would be interesting to compare the positive effects of water therapy on autistic children with the benefits of 'holding sessions', the method used by some therapists such as Dr Martha Welsh in New York. In these sessions the mother holds her autistic child for quite a long time and does everything she can to meet the child's gaze. In one case the child relearns how to communicate directly with its mother. In the other method this is effected through the intermediary of water, symbol of the mother. So why not use both together in the treatment of autistic children?

At the Hanblecěya Therapy Center in California, complete immersion, with a snorkel, is employed to bring about a deep state of regression. This therapy is mostly used for psychotic adults.

Still more unusual is the regressive therapy promoted by the Belgian Dr Karl Ringoet, 'the swimming shrink'. Ringoet is both a psychoanalyst and a diving instructor. He claimed to have cured schizophrenics by using the strange combination of scuba-diving and psychoanalysis. The diving patient is led to a kind of under-water marquee that is supposed to be a grand imitation of a uterus. Underwater speakers produce the sounds that the foetus probably hears in the uterus: the mother's heart and intestinal sounds, the pulsation of the umbilical cord and the filtered voice of the mother. According to Ringoet, the patient needs to learn to feel comfortable in water and to survive under water.

At Cagnes-sur-Mer on the French Riviera, Anne-Marie Saurel uses a kind of artificial womb as a tool for therapy. She has a womb-like room in which there is a bath. When the child is in this bath, preferably with his mother, the light is bluish and from the loudspeakers comes either some music by Mozart or his mother's voice, filtered in such a way that only the frequencies above 8,000 hertz emerge, following Alfred Tomatis's method. Tomatis claims these are the frequencies the baby can perceive while in the womb (only sounds are used in his method of therapy). At the end of the session, when the child shows he wants to get out of the bath, he often sits on his mother's lap in a foetal position, where he is caressed, massaged and wrapped in warm towels. After a certain number of sessions like this, they decide to do a 'sonic delivery', which is set off by stopping the filtered sounds. Saurel observed that the behaviour of the child after the 'sonic delivery' depended on what his actual birth had been like.

One cannot talk about the therapeutic power of water without mentioning jacuzzis. Candido Jacuzzi, an Italian living in California, was an expert in fluid dynamics. He invented the whirlpool bath to treat his grandson, who suffered from rheumatoid arthritis. The jacuzzi is now presented as a way 'to turn your English bathroom into a Continental spring' or 'to replace the household bathtub with an indoor spa'. It is a prime example of how artificial is the distinction between the therapeutic power of water, the erotic power, and water as an utilitarian substance.

Water-beds first became the vogue in the United States at the time of the hippie movement, when sexual liberation was 'in'. Water-beds are now enjoying a new surge of popularity, as it is claimed they are good for bad backs. There are even tiny water-beds specially made for premature babies.

The power of water can be used in subtle ways. Colour therapists recommend a blue or turquoise environment to induce a sense of calm. Naturally, blue or turquoise water has exactly this effect. The healing power of sand is used by some therapists such as Gisela Schuback De Domenico in California. Children are given a tray and play with sand, water and small toys. De Domenico claims that during this 'play therapy' a surprising number of children focus on healing traumatic sequelae that occurred during life in the womb and the period of birth. Sand as a symbol cannot be dissociated from water.

In every place, in every age, there have been endlessly diverse ways to use the therapeutic power of water for every manifestation of ill health or for cultivating good health. And there are new ways adapted to our current society.

In San Francisco it is becoming fashionable to be a 'waterist': that is, to make frequent pilgrimages to 'water bars'. While sitting on a beanbag gazing at a silent television projecting waves on the shore, you are offered a bottle of any type of domestic or imported water. In an aesthetic environment, away from noisy nightclubs or hectic lives, you can choose some Vichy Water from France, or the Italian Ferrarelle, or San Pellegrino Chinotto . . .

A British team in Warwick is trying to perfect a therapy whose aim is to re-create memories of the seaside. Patients are encouraged to relax by sunbathing under an infra-red lamp and listening to a recording of crying gulls, murmuring surf and the distant sound of children playing. A fragrance cassette, blending the smells of fish, seaweed, ozone and a judicious *soupçon* of pollutants, enhances the treatment! Nobody knows what the future of this therapy may be, but the point is the place given to the sense of smell, to odours that lie under the surface of conscious awareness. Why not bring such cassettes into the birthing rooms of our hospitals?

A New Medical Era

The power of water helps us understand the shift towards a new medical era, an era when therapies will be less and less specific and the role of conventional medicine will be more and more confined to the rescue of people in danger.

The period in the history of medicine that is just ending can be described as 'nosologic': the priority is to classify diseases, give them names, and to distinguish one from another, in other words to make diagnoses. The implication is that for each disease, there is a specific treatment. A disease is an imbalance, compared with the equilibrium of good health. Conventional medicine tends to replace one imbalance with another that is considered more comfortable in the short term, and suppresses symptoms at the cost of side effects. This type of medicine might be called 'allo-static'. It is the kind of medicine that treats high blood-pressure with anti-hypertensive drugs, rheumatism with anti-inflammatory drugs, depression with anti-depressant drugs, and so on.

'Nouvelle medicine' perceives a unity between the different aspects of ill health. First, there is a unity between the different situations that create disease. A typical situation that causes illness is submission, or 'helplessness and hopelessness'. This is what happens when, faced with some threat, all one can do is submit. It is impossible to fight or flee. The symptoms and how the disease progresses will differ according to how old the person was when he had to face this situation, how intense the experience was and how long it lasted, as well as many other factors, including genetics. Examples of situations that create disease are when a baby is separated from its mother, a child is raised in an atmosphere of rigid morality, one spouse is dominated by the other, a person loses someone they love, a prisoner is tortured, and so on.

There is a certain unity between the physiological imbalances created by all these situations. Certain hormones, such as cortisol, are secreted at a high level. Certain metabolic pathways are particularly vulnerable to these hormonal secretions – for example, the metabolic pathway of unsaturated fatty acids, which leads to the synthesis of the cell regulators called prostaglandins and plays an important role in the building of the cell membranes. The result is an imbalance between the three series of prostaglandins. This imbalance is almost always tipped one way: usually an excess of prostaglandins series 2.

In the same way one can begin to perceive some possible unity in the way diseases are treated. Nouvelle medicine considers disease, the state of imbalance at a time of crisis, as the body's way of making an effort to heal itself. The new medicine respects this special equilibrium, this effort to heal, as much as possible. It is a 'homoeostatic' medicine. First, it does its best to satisfy those needs created by the critical situation, without losing sight of some basic human needs. Even the word 'therapy' loses its common meaning and just retains its original meaning of 'assistance'. *The aim is to create the best possible circumstances to overcome the crisis.* The idea that we have to have a precise diagnosis before we can do anything is thrown out the window.

Here, for example, is some nutritional advice, in a book written for sufferers of multiple sclerosis. Reduce as much as possible your consumption of animal fat (saturated fat) and of processed oils. Have a high intake of unsaturated fatty acids, mostly from plants and seeds. Supplement your diet with essential fatty acids (contained in, for example, evening primrose oil and fish oils). Take vitamins and minerals such as vitamin C, vitamin B6 and zinc, which act as catalysts in the main metabolic pathways. Stop eating sugar, etc., etc. In fact, this nutritional advice is also perfectly relevant for people with cardiovascular disorders, premenstrual syndrome, skin diseases, rheumatoid arthritis, viral diseases, cancer, depression, anorexia nervosa, etc.

The time has come not to separate these diseases but to understand what they all have in common.

The starting point of this new homoeostatic medicine is to make sure that fundamental needs are met. Take social needs. If the individual is not integrated into a community, he needs substitutes for the extended family, such as therapy groups. There are also some basic human needs that are as old as mankind but forgotten, such as the need to sing. The therapeutic effect of singing is now being rediscovered. Homoeostatic medicine understands that certain emotional states such as faith and hope can work wonders by reversing the effects of submission. Hope and faith can inhibit the secretions of hormones that block the most vulnerable metabolic reactions.

Allostatic medicine is masculine, symbolized by Aesculapius. Homoeostatic medicine is feminine, maternal, symbolized by Hygeia and Panacea. It recognizes that in a crisis people have a special need for a mother.

The therapeutic environment of the future might become more and more feminine. The Aesculapian era of medicine has not extinguished the therapeutic power of water as a feminine symbol. Water helps do away with those barriers that artificially separate different diseases; it also helps us understand the unity between the erotic and the healing powers of water.

Water has a therapeutic power in so far as it is a catalyst to our need to survive. The need to survive and the process of healing are part and parcel of the same thing. Likewise, the need to survive as an individual cannot be dissociated from the need to survive as a species, in other words it cannot be dissociated from Eros.

CHAPTER 6
Religion

Just as it is artificial to separate erotic forces and the process of healing, so it is artificial to separate healing and the religious instinct.

Healing and Religion

In most societies religion and medicine are indistinguishable. Shamanism is as old as mankind. Whether a man or a woman, the shaman has always been both a religious leader and a healer. He or she is a powerful and charismatic personality. Communication with a divine being and the process of healing are indivisible. Things are basically the same in modern industrialized countries. Lourdes became reputed for its healing powers after St Bernadette had seen several visions of the Virgin Mary. Interestingly enough, there is a spring of water in the grotto where Bernadette had seen the Virgin.

Nowadays there are thousands of healers who consider their powers a gift from God. They believe they can show a connection between a patient's healing powers and divine power. Most of these are non-denominational. Others belong to new religious movements often referred to as sects or cults. Usually what these movements have in common is a powerful, authoritarian leader. Other healers follow whatever the prevailing religion may be, particularly Christianity. Christ himself was a healer. There have always been priest–healers. Nowadays some Anglican priests, following Roy Lawrence, openly proclaim that healing is part of their ministry. They remind us that Christian healing started with obedience to Christ, who called on his disciples to heal the sick as well as to proclaim the Gospel. Generally the current resurgence of healers cannot be separated from a new spiritual climate.

When you realize the extent to which religion and medicine have always been bound up together, and when you are aware of the therapeutic power of water, the close relationship between water and religion comes as no surprise.

Water and Religion

An oceanic feeling, a sense of unity with the cosmos – isn't the origin of such feelings our universe when we were foetuses, in amniotic fluid? Here lies a common interpretation of how the religious sense originated. The religious instinct corresponds to a vision of the universe that is inscribed on to the primitive brain, the brain that is already developed during foetal life. This is why the religious instinct is universal. This is why there will always be a religious instinct as long as there are humans who struggle for survival.

Just as the therapeutic power of water has been strong enough to withstand a long allostatic medical era in which diseases are classified, so too has there been a religious revival despite the multiplication of secular states and also of states with official anti-religious propaganda. The religious instinct, channelled by different Churches, is still strong enough today to play a role in various different wars and conflicts.

But it is outside the established Churches that the religious sense tends to express itself more and more. There are a growing number of people who are moving in spiritual directions that have nothing to do with the teachings of any orthodox religion. The religious instinct can show itself in a multitude of ways, so that it is not always recognized for what it is. What is that force that fired me to search for a unity between eroticism, healing and the religious sense? What is that force that fired me to search for a unity between diseases that, on the face of it, have nothing in common? My primitive brain, base for the religious sense, pushed me to make the synthesis, while it was my neocortex that pushed me to analyse, separate and classify.

Whether you are talking about eroticism, the process of healing or the religious sense, water acts as a mediator in all of them. All religions have used the power of water. There is no paradise without water. The Garden of Eden had four rivers flowing through it. There have always been sacred rivers, like the Ganges. In the most ancient religion we know of, the Sumerian religion, the great mother–goddess Inanna has a vase in place of a heart. From this vase flows water that promises eternal spring. The ancient Druids, the Celtic priestly class, conducted their rituals near sacred springs.

Monotheistic religions, which have an image of one Father/God, gained ascendancy in parallel with patriarchal societies. Although predominantly masculine, they channel the universal religious sense by using water, a female image, as the basic symbol.

In many religions, water is first given the power of purification. This explains many customs connected with the age-old human dream of making sex clean in spite of the facts of anatomy, such as the ritual baths that Jewish women must have after menstruating and before their wedding. The ceremonial ablutions performed by Muslims before praying probably have the same meaning. Purification and cleansing are not so easy to differentiate.

In the Christian religion, it is generally agreed that Christ's mission began with his baptism at the age of thirty in the waters of the river Jordan. Getting out of the water is the symbol of a new beginning, a new birth, a passage from death to life. The symbol of the water of baptism has lasted for centuries. It has something in common with the symbolism of holy water and indeed with the use of water in many rites of initiation.

The Kabbalistic rite of transmission of the name of God from master to pupil took place over water. Before the master teaches it to his pupil, they must both immerse themselves. The master says a prayer ending with the words: 'The voice of God is over the waters! Praised be thou, O Lord, who revealest Thy secret to those who fear Thee, He who knoweth Thy mysteries.' Then both must turn their eyes towards the water and recite verses from the Psalms, praising God over the waters.

All through the Bible one finds water. In some cases water is synonymous with fear, danger, hostility or death: 'The Lord overthrew the Egyptians in the midst of the sea . . . and Israel saw the Egyptians dead upon the sea-shore.' Other times water is good and makes life possible, like an oasis in the desert; or it is life-enhancing, like a fountain in a garden or dewdrops on leaves. In the stories of Rebecca, Rachal and the Samaritan, the Bible gives some importance to meetings near wells.

It could be said that the life of Moses is a story about water from start to finish. Probably following a famine, the people of Israel settled in Egypt, where they were victimized. The Pharoah gave the order to throw all new-born baby boys into the river. Moses's mother hid her baby boy for three months and then put him in a basket among the reeds on the river's edge. The Pharoah's daughter rescued the baby from the water and adopted him. So, paradoxically, Moses was saved by the water. When Moses grew up, it was near a well that he met his wife, the daughter of a tribal chief who taught him where to find water in the desert. When the Israelites decided to go back to their own country, God led them towards the Red Sea. But they were trapped between the sea and the Egyptian army. Moses spread his hand upon the sea and the waters divided and the children of Israel could walk on the dried sea-bed with a wall of water to their left and right. When the Egyptian army chased after them, Moses spread his hand again. The sea closed up and the Egyptians drowned. After this episode there was a time when the children of Israel encamped in Reph-idim, and there was no water for the people to drink. Moses followed the order of God, smote the rock in Horeb, and water flowed out of it.

The victorious crossing through the anxieties of the sea is a key event in the Judaeo-Christian faiths. It signalled the passage from a state of servitude to a state of freedom. This episode also underlies the mysterious nature of water. It reminds us that faith feeds on mysteries.

Mystery – A Need

Here again water brings together faith, healing and eroticism. What they have in common is a need for mystery.

Doctors have always known that mystery helps the healing

process. Until recently, they used to talk in Latin, a language mysterious to lay people. By comparison, modern medical language is an easy jargon to decode. When I was a surgeon, I was aware that there was a certain therapeutic power inherent in the procedures of a surgeon. The surgeon hidden behind his mask, working in a 'no admittance' area, having access to the insides of anaesthetized human bodies, followed a sort of religious ritual. This has always stimulated the imagination, especially at a time when the surgeon still belonged to a rare species.

These days, doctors have lost some of their aura of mystery. Perhaps they have lost some of their effectiveness at the same time. Alternative practitioners know what to do to cultivate mystery, and they have a whole variety of ways of doing it. For example, they use techniques that started out in distant countries, and distant things are always mysterious. Or else they use techniques whose theoretical bases are unclear, and therefore charged with mystery.

In the same way eroticism has always fed on mystery. Marriages always took place between different clans or tribes, rather than within the clan or tribe. The behaviour of boys and girls reared together in Israeli kibbutzim has been studied. Up to the age of twelve, heterosexual games are common in the dormitories. But at puberty the girls tend to reject the boys and want their own bedrooms and showers. They become hostile to the boys of their community ... but, at the same time, they start making eyes at boys who belong to other groups. Nowadays, with modern means of communication, the attraction between partners who don't share the same country of origin, or the same language, or who don't belong to the same race, is obvious.

It has been claimed that eroticism is the art of concealing some skin, thereby maintaining a certain mystery. This is a point that Darwin did not take into consideration when interpreting the nakedness of humans. Darwin questioned the advantages of losing hair during the process of evolution, and came to see hair loss as a decorative advantage, in other words an advantage in terms of sexual attraction. There are also decorative reasons why humans replace hair by clothes. The atmosphere is more erotic at a masked ball than at a nudist camp.

One can ask why, for thousands of years, women hid themselves away from the sight of men when giving birth. For thousands of years the world of women and the phenomenon of birth was mysterious to men, just as the feats of the warriors and hunters were mysterious to women. When the extent to which sexual attraction needs mystery is realized, it is possible to understand the societies that came before ours more easily. The New York psychiatrist Sam Janus found that 30 per cent of men who had been present at the birth of their children later lost sexual interest in their wives. Generally speaking, it is difficult to cultivate mystery inside a monogamous nuclear family.

Some educators have understood the importance of water as a powerful intermediary of mystery. Maria Montessori considered that the first aim of the teacher should be to maintain a constant state of curiosity and to stimulate the imagination. She was aware of the need for mystery. In order to 'sow the seeds of the sciences' among children, she suggested that water should become a point of departure. She showed how the cosmic plan can be presented to the child as a thrilling tale of the earth we live on, with the many changes through slow ages 'when water was Nature's chief toiler for the accomplishment of her purposes'. Because one can look at water from different points of view, its study 'can become a passion'. 'One would like to be able to penetrate the mysteries and the majesty inherent in water.' Montessori knew not only that water is a mediator for mystery, but also that it is, itself, a mystery.

Water – A Mystery

For scientists, water remains a mystery. All substances become heavier, denser, when they turn from liquid into solid. But it is the opposite with water: ice floats. If it were not so, ice would fall to the cold bottom of the sea and, winter after winter, more and more water would turn into ice.

Another example. A compressed liquid usually becomes more viscous. It is the opposite with water, which becomes more slippery as long as the temperature is below 40°C.

Scientists are penetrating deeper and deeper into the mysteries

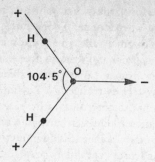

of this miraculous molecule, which makes life possible. It is better and better understood that without water the elements essential to life would never come together. Even at the molecular level, water plays the role of a mediator, an agent of unification. The powerful intermolecular forces in water are caused by the specific 'bizarre' distribution of electrons in the molecule.

From spectroscopic and X-ray analysis, the precise H-O-H bond angle is 104.5°. This arrangement of electrons in the molecule gives it electric asymmetry. When two molecules approach each other closely, there is an electrostatic attraction between the negative charge on the oxygen atom of one molecule and the positive charge on the hydrogen atom of an adjacent molecule. This creates a redistribution of the electronic charges in both molecules that greatly enhances their attraction. This complex electrostatic union is called the 'hydrogen bond'. Because of the special arrangement of the electrons, each water molecule is potentially capable of hydrogen bonding with four neighbouring water molecules. This explains the great internal cohesion of water.

What makes water so mysterious is that there is no pure water, no unique model of water. The fragile architecture of water can be modified according to the temperature, the pressure and the electromagnetic radiation. Modern methods of investigation suggest that there is not one unique form of water, but many different forms that are combined in different ways. Depending on whether the molecules are isolated, or associated by groups of two, three, four or five, the water is called monomere, dimere, trimere, tetramere or pentamere. If some OH^- or OH^+ ions are released, water is ionized.

According to the proportion of all these different forms, one might say that every water has its own personality. For example, rain-water, storm-water or water under a full moon do not have the same spectrum.

Our modern understanding of the fragile architecture of water does not go against the popular belief in many cultures that it acts as a link between earth and the cosmos. Some customs still practised reveal a knowledge about the changing quality of water according to the changing sky. It is the custom in many cultures not to hang out washing when there is a full moon. From a chemical perspective, full-moon water can be particularly aggressive. In certain regions of the Himalayas all the reservoirs must be emptied before and after an eclipse.

Water, that mysterious and miraculous molecule, continues to astonish many scientists. Some of them are now saying that water has a memory. It is as if water can record its history in its physical structure. Luu, in Montpellier, using a Raman-Laser spectrometer, showed that water that has contained a substance will retain a characteristic spectrum, even when it has been diluted so much that a chemist would be unable to find a trace of the original substance.

At Salford University in England, Cyril Smith studied the effects of electromagnetic fields on water. He proposed a helical structure for water that is capable of 'remembering' frequencies to which it has been exposed. More recently the French biologist Jacques Benveniste put his professional credibility at stake by publishing tests in the prestigious journal *Nature* that suggested a tendency for water to 'remember' molecules with which it had been in contact. Benveniste claimed that some blood cells can respond to antibodies for dilutions up to 1 on 1 followed by 120 zeros! The editor could not 'believe the unbelievable' and was anxious to protect the reputation of the journal. A week-long visit in the French laboratory by *Nature*'s team (including a magician recruited to watch out for possible trickery!) concluded that there was no conscious fraud but probably some unintentional errors. What a good conclusion to cultivate mystery!

The concept of 'structured water' is introducing a new vision of living tissues. According to theories that are supported by some of Tcharkovsky's scientific advisers, water in living beings is divided into two types: the water forming hydrogen bonds with cellular structures, and the free water in which the hydrogen bonds are formed between water molecules only. The human body is a dynamic liquid crystal composed of approximately 70 per cent 'structurized' water. We are rediscovering what ancient cultures knew. In Egypt and China they used to recognize the influence on human health of lunar cycles (gravitational fields), specific metals and crystal structures (electromagnetic fields), and plant and animal matter (bioenergetic fields).

Inspired by these theories, underwater birth aims to use the ability of 'structured water' to 'store and communicate' certain bioenergetic information to a living being in it. Igor Smirnov, from Leningrad, claims the water in the tank in which childbirth will take place should first be treated – that is to say, 'structured' – for twelve hours before labour and also during labour. A special 'biogenerator' has been created for this purpose.

Water is not only mysterious to all those scientists who study it at molecular level, but also to those who study its shape. Leonardo da Vinci is considered to be the first man to make systematic experiments with water in the modern sense of the word. He perceived the wonders of this element and its relationship with living beings in the course of their development.

Some people have been fascinated by the tendency of all flowing water to follow a meandering course. It is as if water is always trying to make a circle, but is only partially successful because of the force of gravity. Even within meanders there are secondary currents with a circular sort of action, fascinating in their complexity. The meeting of two such currents can cause a spiralling movement. The loops become so pronounced that a flood can cause them to be by-passed and left as backwaters.

The simple observation of meanders is enough to reveal certain mysteries. Water has a constant tendency to re-create a sphere.

There is a constant conflict between this tendency and the force of gravity. This explains meanders, spirals, backwaters, and so on. This also leads us to a new vision of a drop of water: a rain-drop is a sphere stretched by gravity.

Water constantly tries to re-create a sphere, that is to say, a whole, a unity. Water constantly seeks to put together that which is divided. Whether the approach is chemical, physical or symbolic, water always seems to be the mediator, the link, the element that binds things and people together. Mediation, relation, religion . . .

CHAPTER 7
Man and Dolphin

Six centuries before Christ, Aesop illustrated the very special relationship between men and dolphins in a fable, 'The Ape and the Dolphin'. He told the story of a shipwreck. Among the sailors there was an ape. A dolphin mistook the ape for a man and began to carry him on his back towards the shore. Discovering his mistake on the way, the dolphin allowed the ape to drown. In this fable, Aesop showed his awareness of the close relationship between humans and apes, long before zoologists classified us among the primates. Putting himself in the place of a sea mammal, he knew that such a mistake was possible. But at the same time Aesop demonstrated his knowledge of a special relationship between humans and dolphins. We'll use this fable as a starting point for a triangular study of the common points and differences between apes, humans and sea mammals.

There are innumerable studies comparing humans and apes, including studies of fossils, anatomy, physiology and behaviour. All those who have tried to determine the time when the hominids separated from the apes relied on the differences between humans and other primates.

There are fewer studies comparing humans and sea mammals, and they are more anecdotal. They often concentrate on one particular point, such as the brain, or more precisely the neocortex, with the aim of assessing the intelligence of sea mammals. The main aim is rarely to improve our understanding of the human phenomenon. However, we can probably learn a lot about human nature from comparisons with sea mammals.

As time goes on, more and more voices proclaim the close

relationship between humans and sea mammals. Jacques Cousteau wrote that gravity is the original sin. Redemption will come only when we return to the water, as sea mammals did in the past. Tcharkovsky also believes that human beings are mammals ready to go back to an aquatic environment.

To the voices of those who wonder whether man is destined to return to the sea, one can add the voices putting this question the other way round: was man more aquatic in the past? Might it not have been in the sea that man learned to stand up? Might it not have been possible that the direct ancestor of man, the missing link, was a primate spending some of its life in water? This last question was raised by Sir Alister Hardy, a professor at Oxford University, in the *New Scientist* in 1960. These questions were asked again and taken further by the writer Elaine Morgan, author of *Descent of Woman* and *The Aquatic Ape*. The study of the ape–man–dolphin triangle that follows owes a great deal to the work of both Sir Alister Hardy and Elaine Morgan.

The method of study I propose is simple. Let us take, one by one, the characteristics that make man an exception among the apes, and let us study these characteristics with reference to the sea mammals.

The Naked Ape

The absence of hair is certainly the most striking difference between man and ape. This is the principal difference noted by Desmond Morris in his famous book *The Naked Ape*, which reminded us that, in spite of our large brain, above all we are primates. This is how the book begins: 'There are one hundred and ninety-three living species of monkeys and apes. One hundred and ninety-two of them are covered with hair. The exception is a naked ape self-named *Homo sapiens*.' Many theories have tried to interpret this peculiarity and the possible advantages in terms of evolution. It has been claimed that for our ancestors the lack of hair was a way to protect themselves against too much heat. But even in the hottest countries there are no examples of hunting mammals that use this method of protection against heat. Nomadic Arabs had to invent the hooded robe called a burnous for this purpose.

Until the last century others suggested that nakedness was the best protection against the many skin parasites found in tropical regions. Darwin rejected this interpretation, saying that if it was the case, other animals living in the tropics would have got rid of their hairy coats to cope with the same problem. Darwin saw the advantages of nudity as a factor in sexual attraction. Ever since, it has been emphasized that in the field of sexual attraction the species always takes advantage of the exaggeration of some of their characteristic features, rather than their disappearance. It has also been argued that naked skin makes sexual activity more pleasurable and so creates a stronger attachment between the members of the couple. But, in fact, it is doubtful whether a high sensibility to erotic stimuli reinforces the pair bond and the tendency to monogamy.

Let us now turn to a comparison between humans and cetaceans (dolphins, whales and porpoises). The absence of hair is a characteristic of most sea mammals. The only ones that keep their fur are those that can get out of the water and stay on land in a cold climate, such as seals, otters and beavers. It is obvious that fur can protect from differences of temperature in so far as it can maintain a layer of air around the body. It is interesting to note that man has lost his hair practically everywhere except on his head – the only part of his body that is above the water when he swims. In fact, it is not strictly true that man has no hair. In the Caucasian races there is an almost invisible down covering most of the body. But when it comes to the resistance to the water when swimming, it makes no difference if hair has disappeared completely, as in some black races, or whether there are still vestiges of hair.

It is very interesting to study the directions of this down's growth on different parts of the body. It is not the same in man as it is in apes. On the back of a human, the down goes diagonally, as if to meet the down on the other side of the median line. This is exactly the direction it would be induced to take if a man was swimming like a frog, and the water was sliding off the skin. This arrangement is particularly striking in the foetus, which is covered in down called lanugo. Usually this hair disappears before birth, or sometimes just after birth. Some scientists have argued that the nakedness of man was nothing other than the persistence of characteristics special to the foetus and the baby, carried over into adult life (the process of neoteny). However, the fact that lanugo exists and then disappears flies in the face of this interpretation. The disappearance of hair in man seems to be indistinguishable from the presence of a layer of subcutaneous fat and the development of sweat glands.

The Fatty Ape

With his layer of fat under the skin, man is an exception among the primates. Apes also have some fat; however, it is not under the skin but mostly around the internal organs of the abdomen. This fat's only function is to serve as an energy reserve. When an orang-utan in captivity becomes obese, he has a big belly but no fat under the skin of his cheeks, thighs or fingers. If you wanted to have a look at the fat cells that make a chimpanzee's skin supple, you would need a microscope.

On the other hand, a layer of subcutaneous fat is common to all mammals that are adapted to water. This layer of fat protects them against the cold. It also makes them more buoyant. Their bodies are more streamlined, more 'aquadynamic'. This characteristic of human beings appears at a very early age. Compared with the chubby human baby, the baby ape is thin and bony. If he was like an ape, the human baby would not weigh much more than four pounds at birth. It is perhaps on the question of babies that subcutaneous fat gives us most to think about. Indeed, at this age food in the form of milk is guaranteed for several months and there is no need to build up reserves.

When you look at the human being as a primate adapted to water, the meaning of nakedness and subcutaneous fat ceases to be mysterious. The skin and the subcutaneous fat of the *Hippopotamus amphibius* together weigh 450 kg!

The Perspiring Ape

There is also some significance in sweat, which has puzzled many scientists. Man has been called 'the perspiring primate'; he is a primate who earns his living 'by the sweat of his brow'. Perhaps in this phrase from Genesis the literal meaning of the word 'sweat' is sometimes overlooked. Body temperature-control through the loss of sweat has often been considered to be a biological blunder. It is a costly mechanism, depleting the system of large amounts of water, sodium and other essential elements. This makes no sense whatsoever for those who consider the human being to be a primate who keeps the characteristics of a foetus or a baby at the age of adulthood. In fact, the human baby does not control its temperature by sweating for the first few weeks following birth.

The skin of an adult human can lose huge quantities of sweat. His skin is endowed with one hundred and fifty to four hundred sweat glands, called eccrine glands, per square centimetre. The ape's much sparser eccrine glands respond to emotion but not to heat. Other species that apparently sweat, such as horses, are using their scent signalling glands.

New interpretations become possible if you think of the human being as a primate adapted to environments where water and minerals are available without restriction.

The Two-legged Ape

There is another difference that anyone can immediately see between man and ape, and indeed between man and other land-based mammals: man is upright and walks on two legs. Many people have asked why, originally, man adopted this unstable and tiring position that puts him into a constant conflict with gravity.

Certainly, the upright position has the advantage of leaving the hands free to use tools or weapons. It also enables us to look into the distance. But one still has to ask how it was possible to abandon being on all fours, which made movement fast and safe on many kinds of terrain.

One might also claim that our adaptation to the upright position is not perfect. A difficult and incomplete adaptation to the upright position is the only possible interpretation for some pathological conditions that are specific to humans. Hernias of the groin might be considered as the price to be paid for being on two legs. Hernias are common in humans but unknown in veterinary medicine. When I was practising surgery, I had a special interest in hernias. The fact that they happen only in humans influenced my strategy as a surgeon. I made a short film based on the idea that the aim of the operation should not be simply to repair the hernia; rather the region should be built another way – rebuilt. Back pain brings millions of patients to doctors and therapists every day. Once again, it amounts to a specifically human pathological condition brought about by imperfect adaptation to being upright.

Let's now compare human beings with sea animals, and we'll have a new vision of two-leggedness.

Think of penguins. Either they are on land and have a quasi-human gait that is not common among birds, or they are swimming horizontally with their limbs aligned with the body, like humans. For many sea mammals, being vertical in the water is a favourite posture when they are near the shore or when their curiosity is awakened. This is what domestic dolphins do when they are waiting for food or for orders from their trainer. It's the same for dugongs and manatees when the mother is breast-feeding her babies. It's obvious that a primate adapted to water tends to hold himself upright, so as to be able to walk further without getting out of his depth.

Generally speaking, whether in an upright or horizontal position, the spine of sea mammals is aligned with the hind limbs. Here is an essential point in common between humans and cetaceans. Adaptation to water goes with great flexibility of the spine, which is another peculiarity of humans compared with apes, and another point in common between humans and cetaceans. Thanks to the great flexibility of the spine, some humans can cover a distance of a hundred metres in less than a minute by swimming in a butterfly style, using the legs in a dolphin-like kick. There is no example of an ape that can bend backwards.

The Orgasmic Ape

Humans are also different from all other primates in the way they make love. With apes, and even with land-based quadrupeds, the male mounts the female from behind. In all human cultures, the most common position is face to face, even if other positions are possible and practised. The face-to-face position is the best one for the direction of the vagina leaning towards the front. A lot has been said about the possible correlation between face-to-face copulation and monogamy. Face-to-face copulation seems to go with the stimulation of a great number of erogenous zones. This position, by making the body contact as close and as intimate as possible, would enhance the attachment between sexual partners and cement the relationship. These questions are topical at a time when scientists are trying to get to the bottom of what might be the physiological basis for attachment within a couple. Both partners secrete a large amount of opiates, of endorphins, during sexual intercourse. A quality of opiates is to trigger habits of dependency. When you realize that, you observe that close body-to-body contact, together with a high level of endorphins, might be the beginning of a habit, in other words a bond cementing the couple together. The attachment between members of a couple has as its model the bond between mother and baby. Both mother and baby have a high level of endorphins immediately after birth and probably after breast-feeding as well.

These questions are particularly relevant at a time when scientists can perceive some biological advantages of monogamy – or, at least, monoandry – among humans. It seems that when a woman has the same man father all her children, to a certain extent she runs less risk of having a miscarriage, toxaemia and pre-eclampsia. Some miscarriages can be prevented by artificially creating the situation of a woman who has had several children with the same man: the immune system of the woman is prepared with some white cells of the father-to-be that she receives as an injection before becoming pregnant.

Things are not simple, however, and some members of the monkey family (gibbons, marmosets and indris, who do not copulate face to face), rather than humans, are the most monogamous primates. What these animals have in common is their low sex drive.

Once more, what makes man an exception among the primates is the rule among cetaceans. From the many descriptions of sea mammals mating, it seems that it always happens face to face, with the exception of seals and sea-lions when they are on the shore. Not only do these descriptions give interesting facts about the position, but they also suggest that the female, as well as the male, can reach a real orgasmic state. Victor Schaffer, describing the mating of whales, wrote: 'At the end the pair rise high above the sea, black snouts against the sky.' This has been expressed poetically by Heathcote Williams:

> With a last movement,
> Powerfully churning their flukes in unison fifty feet below,
> They propel themselves upwards,
> Gallons of water sluicing down their sides,
> They both jump clear,
> Held together, in mid-air, for their massive climax.

And R. M. Martin on the subject of dolphins wrote: 'What seems like real love is transmitted between the two participating individuals.' This shared ecstasy might be another thing in common between humans and cetaceans. Have humans been made more orgasmic thanks to the power of water? Women, unlike female apes, can have sexual intercourse all through their menstrual cycle. This is another point in common with female dolphins, who make love several times a day, all the year round, even if they are not in 'heat'.

Dolphins have incredibly active sex lives. They masturbate from an early age and pursue promiscuous homosexual and heterosexual contacts that seem to be purely social. It has been claimed that the great number of sexual activities unconnected with reproductive goals is correlated with the large brain and the expanded neocortex.

In the Sind, a province of Pakistan in the lower Indus Valley, the female dolphin is a sexual symbol. A nymphomaniac woman is called a *bulhan*, which is a variety of freshwater dolphin. According to a legend, the first *bulhan* was born from a woman who used to make love with dolphins. The local troubadours still celebrate the Indus, the dolphins and love all together.

This comparison of the sexual behaviour of humans and sea mammals reveals the importance of recent observations of a very special ape, the pygmy chimpanzee, or bonobo. This ape is not well known by scientists, because it lives in the flooded and thick forests of Zaire. Recently Frans de Waal from the San Diego Zoo published some valuable documents. Photos demonstrate that the bonobos commonly copulate face to face, and that they are orgasmic. One can see an orgasmic female showing her teeth during sexual intercourse in the missionary position. A high-pitched sound has been heard during the paroxysm. It is noticeable that the vulva of the bonobo is oriented towards the front, as is the human one. These apes have a great amount of sexual activity. They have sexual contacts with any partner, male or female, of whatever age, and in any position. In other words, they can have sexual activity quite independent from reproductive goals.

Apparently Frans de Waal does not make any correlation between the very special behaviour of the bonobo and other reasons why this ape had already been considered as 'an uncommon chimp': it is an aquatic ape. The pygmy chimp spends part of its time wading in water and catching fish. On the other hand, those who have been puzzled by the special relationship of this ape with water were probably not aware of its unusual sexual behaviour. What makes this chimp a key for a better understanding of humans is the correlation between these two kinds of behavioural features; face-to-face copulation and spectacular orgasms cannot be dissociated from the adaptation to water.

The Weeping Ape

Tears are the symbol of human emotions. It is through tears that Mary Magdalene saw the resurrected Jesus. Tears are always given a special status compared with all the other body secretions. In her book about breast-feeding, Ina May Gaskin, the well-known American midwife, humorously summarizes the common human attitude towards tears: 'If you watch network television for a couple of days, you could easily get the idea that tears are the only socially acceptable secretion of the human body, provided that they are shed only by women and very young children.'

I.

Labour in water

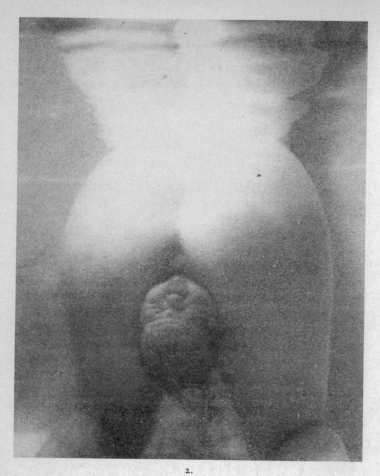

2.

Birth under water

3.

Welcoming baby: a mother and her sister
(*opposite, top*)

4.

Welcoming baby
(*opposite, below*)

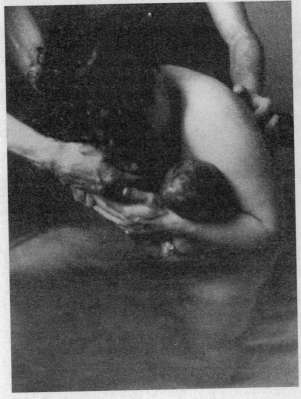

5.
A Wedding Scene, Niccolò di Segna (twelfth century)

6.
The Birth of Venus, Sandro Botticelli (1485)

7.

Apollo meets Thetis, a daughter of the god of the sea.
The Setting of the Sun, François Boucher (eighteenth century)

8.
The
water-attracted
ape

Yet again, man is the exception. He is the only primate who floods his eyes to express certain feelings. Although a chimpanzee can express a wide range of emotions, you'll never see a tear in his eye. Here once again is an enigma difficult to resolve when you compare man only with other terrestrial animals. But this enigma is solved immediately as soon as you look at the sea mammals: tear glands and other salt glands mean adaptation to the sea. Freshwater crocodiles do not shed tears, whereas marine crocodiles do. Land lizards do not cry, but the lizards of the tropical seas, the iguanas, do.

All sea birds have big nasal glands that secrete large quantities of salt liquid, the equivalent of tears. Human tears also flow out through the nose. It is only during some special emotional states, or when the tear duct is obstructed, that our eyes are flooded. The tears of sea mammals have been particularly studied in seals and otters. When a mother sea otter is separated from her baby, she cries like a human mother.

Of course the excretory function of the human tear gland is negligible, but it serves as a vestige of this function and gives scientists some idea of man's place in the animal world. Our kidneys have the glomerulus to protect us against too much water and too much salt and the tubules to protect us against too little water and too little salt. For marine animals the priority is to eliminate excess salt. With their huge concentration of salt, tears can be interpreted in no other way than as signs of adaptation to the sea. Even if the excretory function of tears is negligible in practice, it is worth pointing out that the composition of tears brought on by an irritating substance like an onion is different from that brought on by emotions (there is a smaller amount of stress hormones). Tears have been used as a simple and non-invasive way to quantify hormonal wastes.

The Water-attracted Ape

Every year in summer, on every continent, on the coasts of every ocean and every sea, millions of human beings spend whole days looking at the water, or paddling in it, or playing in the waves.

There are a multitude of ways in which human beings show

they are attracted to water. The young child who wants to do the washing-up with his mother is just using that as an excuse to play with water. All aquatic sports are popular, both to watch or participate in, whether it's sailboat races, surfing, windsurfing, water polo or 'aquatics' – a kind of ballet on the borderline between sport and an erotic show.

This attraction to water also differentiates *Homo sapiens* from other apes. In zoos, there is a simple barrier around the territory of chimpanzees or gorillas – a ditch full of water. Among humans, such a ditch has the opposite implication. Water means a way of escaping, escaping from hard reality. Jung knew this when he published *Man and His Symbols*. He told the story of the film *Crin blanc*, which is about a young rider who must escape from a group of hunters to save the wild horse he is riding. When surrounded by the hunters, the young man and his mount escape from reality by disappearing into the sea.

There are exceptions, however. It has been reported that gorillas in zoos have been seen swimming the breaststroke. It is nevertheless significant that an article containing observations of pygmy chimps wading in water and catching fish was entitled 'An Uncommon Chimp'. Other exceptions among monkeys include the Japanese macaques, which have adapted to life on the seashore of an island and are not frightened by water. Interestingly, these water-adapted monkeys are very clever and can transmit tricks to other members of the group; they found a way to wash their potatoes in the sea. One type of Japanese macaque, the 'snow monkeys', discovered that they could get warm by swimming in hot springs.

Humans swim for pleasure. This is not the result of any conditioning by our civilization. The younger a person is, the less he has been subjected to any conditioning, and the more he loves water. Look at young children in a paddling pool. The younger they are, the happier they are. The younger a baby is, the easier it is for him to swim. In the right environment a baby can swim before he can walk. Of course, young human beings have an extraordinary capacity to learn, as long as it is in a joyful atmosphere. This is not exclusive to swimming. Very young children have been taught how to read and how to do 'instant maths'. But this is different from learning to swim. The human baby is perfectly adapted to water at birth. All he needs is the chance to cultivate this adaptation. This was known at the time of the Greeks and Romans, and is common knowledge on some Pacific islands. And it has been rediscovered by a number of swimming teachers.

Not only do human beings have the ability to swim, but Igor Smirnov thinks that those who do so during their early development seem to be ahead of their contemporaries. He carried out an investigation at the No. 10 Children's Policlinic in Leningrad with a group of children who had not been born in water, but who swam regularly from the first days of life. He studied many aspects of their development, including the ability to classify by shape and colour, and the reproduction of monosyllables, and came to the conclusion that the aquatic environment promotes early speech development.

The Diving Ape

Man is a diving primate. This aptitude for diving is not just the result of training: humans are equipped with diving reflexes. If you dip your face in a basin full of water, your heart rate will slow down. This kind of reflex is developed among all animals that dive. For example, the heart rate of penguins is 200 beats per minute in the air and can slow down to 20 when diving. The heart rate of Jacques Mayol, the famous French diver, is usually around 60 beats per minute, but it goes down to 28 when he is 80 metres under the surface. It even went down to 22 during a 50-metre dive in an ice lake in Peru, at an altitude of 5,000 metres. The feats of Mayol are totally exceptional for a human being. He can go down to a depth of 100 metres without oxygen. When a diver can reach a depth of 20 metres unaided and can stay submerged for three minutes, he is considered to have reached the limits of human possibility.

Of course, this is far below the capacities of sea mammals. The record holder for this is the sperm whale, which can descend to 1,000 metres and stay submerged for seventy-five minutes. The physiological mechanisms of adaptation to diving have been best studied in the Weddell seal, which lives on the shores and coastal ice of Antarctica. Perhaps these mechanisms are not basically different from those of humans, but are simply much more developed. This species of seal is able to plunge more than 500 metres and remain under water for more than an hour. Blood represents 14 per cent of the seal's body weight compared with 7 per cent in humans. In the seal's blood is 70 per cent of the oxygen store, compared with 51 per cent in humans. The ratio is 25 per cent and 13 per cent for oxygen stored in the muscles. During a dive, blood is redistributed. When seals are diving, blood continues to be supplied at the normal rate to the retina, brain, spinal cord, adrenal glands and the placenta, whereas the blood flow is shut off to organs such as the kidneys, which stop functioning. It has been demonstrated that the foetal heart rate does slow down when its mother dives, although its diving reflex is slower and less pronounced than its mother's. It is as if the foetus 'knows' its mother is diving.

There is another diving mechanism that usually goes unnoticed, but which is of interest when comparing man, apes and sea mammals: the seal's nostrils are closed when it is under the water. This is a common mechanism of adaptation to water. Among land-based animals, only camels can close their nostrils, in order to keep out sand.

It is significant that one of the only devices used by Mayol when diving is a nose clamp. This is a way of protecting the facial sinuses against excessive pressure. On the face of it, one might think that, as far as the nostrils are concerned, there is hardly a trace of any adaptive mechanism. But one should first note that the other primates have no nostrils at all, except the male proboscis monkey, which is the only semi-aquatic primate. Also it is not totally accurate to claim that the seals close their nostrils to dive. It would be more accurate to say that they open their nostrils when they get out of the water. Some muscles contract to open the nostrils, and just relax to close them. In fact, humans have rudimentary muscles capable of enlarging the nostrils slightly, but when these muscles are completely relaxed the nostrils are not closed. We use this ability to enlarge the nostrils in a subtle way to express certain feelings, such as anger. It is significant that the extinct 'duck-footed' humans called Agaiumbu, who inhabited a lagoon in New Guinea, had huge nostrils that appeared. to dilate and contract, according to a report by C. A. W. Monckton at the beginning of this century.

One can make a connection between the diving abilities of humans and the recent discovery that some people can survive long periods of total immersion without brain damage after re-suscitation. The most spectacular case occurred in 1977, when a young man was brought back to consciousness after thirty-eight minutes under water in Lake Michigan. Mayol likes to refer to this case as evidence of the aquatic adaptation of man.

Humans are endowed with diving physiological control mech-anisms, but they are also fascinated by life under water. It is not by chance that one of the most attractive works of Jules Verne is *Twenty Thousand Leagues under the Sea*, the story of Captain Nemo and his submarine *Nautilus*. Today, thanks to snorkels and other sophisticated devices, we can more easily satisfy our desire to go under water. There are busy full-time diving guides like Dee Scarr, who has been practising in the Bahamas and the Antilles. His programme *Touch the Sea* is a personalized guided dive. Scarr knows when children become curious about underwater life and his book of fantasy, *Coral's Reef*, is about a talking octopus.

It is no exaggeration to say that the age of submarine leisure has dawned. There is now a new generation of undersea tourists thanks to sightseeing submarines, following the trend set by the *Auguste Picard*, which operated in the waters of Lake Geneva during the 1960s. The modern 'Looking-glass' submarines can shoot out jets of fish food to attract marine life. What geniuses were the men who understood that to transmit *joie de vivre* throughout the world you had only to repeat 'We all live in a yellow submarine' – and add a background noise of water.

The Talking Ape

Language is often put forward as the gulf that separates human beings from the animal world. Whether to underline this gulf, or to do the opposite and challenge it as an unsurmountable barrier, the most common approach is to try and push the linguistic capacities of apes to their limits. This has not led to any very spectacular performances. It took six years of unremitting effort for the chimpanzee Vicky to be able to say, rather indistinctly, four words as simple as 'mummy', 'daddy', 'cup' and 'up'. By contrast, the chimpanzee Washoe, like the gorillas Michael and Koko, acquired a much larger vocabulary more quickly by learning the sign language of the deaf. It is well known that apes communicate above all with gestures, attitudes and facial expressions. It is not by chance that in many languages 'to ape' means to imitate through movements and gestures. This does not rule out that apes can sometimes express strong feelings with involuntary, spontaneous vocal signals.

Human communication has not been compared with that of sea mammals to the same extent. Sea mammals mostly communicate with sounds, which is something they have in common with humans. Nowadays it is hard not to believe that dolphins have a genuine language. Not only do they make whistling sounds, but apparently they stay silent in order to listen to another dolphin whistling. When a dolphin starts whistling, other dolphins in the group start to whistle too, but never before the first one has finished. It's as if you never interrupt in the world of dolphins. The ways that dolphins communicate are still mysterious. For example, two dolphins, isolated from each other in different tanks, can convey to each other the trick of how to open the fish store.

Perhaps the dolphins' way of communicating with each other is connected with their ability to know where they are by echoes, like bats do. Maybe they are capable of transmitting true descriptions of objects, exact copies of which they can identify by this system of 'echolocation'. It is possible that dolphins communicate in a way we have not yet understood, or find difficult to understand. It also seems that they can alter their emotional states by means of sounds. The powerful effect of sounds on the emotions might be something in common between humans and cetaceans. Sounds have powerful effects on human beings. The power of sounds can be compared only with the power of water.

Just as the therapeutic power of water has always been used, so too have people always sought the healing power of sounds. Primitive societies give more importance to magical songs in healing the sick than to medicinal plants. Singing and music were therapeutic tools in the medical systems of ancient China, Persia, Egypt and Greece. Hippocrates, the father of medicine, used to bring mental patients to the Temple of Aesculapius to listen to music. Today the therapeutic value of singing and music is being rediscovered by some isolated pioneers. Among them is Marie-Louise Aucher in France, who has devoted her career to developing the therapeutic power of singing. Thanks to her we had singing groups in the maternity unit in Pithiviers Hospital. When these groups started, we were thinking of the vibrations a baby can perceive while in the womb, and also of the emotional balance of the mothers-to-be.

In a similar sort of way, in many cultures all over the world, singing and music were part and parcel of the religious sense. In ancient civilizations any audible sound was considered as a manifestation of one fundamental supraphysic sound, which the Hindus called OM. This primal sound, though inaudible, would be present everywhere as a divine vibration. Churches all over the world have always stimulated the religious sense by singing and music. Western classical music apparently had its origins in medieval religious music. J. S. Bach claimed that music existed to glorify God and improve man. So a great sensitivity to sounds might be another thing humans have in common with dolphins.

Only humans have articulate language. But what is it that makes this possible? Speech means first the capacity to control the respiratory rhythm. And the control of the respiratory rhythm cannot be dissociated from the capacity to dive. Articulate language also means having a descended larynx, that is to say, having the capacity to raise or relax the velum, so that the nasal cavity can be either connected or disconnected from the rest of the respiratory tract. In most mammals the larynx connects directly with the back of the nasal passages. In other words, a channel from nostrils to lungs remains open at all times, so that the mammals can swallow and breathe at the same time. New-born

71

human babies are nose-breathers until they reach the age of three months, when the larynx descends. The descended larynx seems to be a characteristic of all the members of our species. A team from Tel Aviv has reported the discovery of the hyoid bone in a 60,000-year-old Neanderthal skeleton from Kebara Cave on Mount Carmel. When there is a hyoid bone, which anchors eleven important muscles connected to the skull and larynx, it means that the larynx does not connect directly with the nasal passage and that it can be mobilized.

Interestingly enough, water is the only environment in which a permanently open channel from nostrils to lungs ceases to be an advantage. Breathing through the mouth can satisfy an urgent need to inhale large quantities of air instantly before diving or when resurfacing.

The Fish-eating Ape

Attention has often been drawn to the differences in the diet between humans and chimpanzees. Apes live on a diet of fruits and other plants. Humans are omnivorous; they are both hunters and gatherers. It is usual to think of meat-eating as something only humans do in the world of apes. But things are not so simple, and in certain circumstances male chimpanzees can occasionally become hunters and eat flesh, while female chimpanzees can eat small insects such as termites.

There is another aspect of the human diet that is worth mentioning. Humans eat fish and shellfish. Moreover, during the last few years, nutritionists have become aware of the importance of fish and other seafoods in the optimum human diet. This new awareness came about thanks to an increased knowledge of the different fatty acids and their metabolism.

It is now generally agreed that modern man has a tendency to eat too much animal fat. By contrast, he does not eat enough fatty acids of vegetable origin, or else the vegetable oils he does consume have been processed in some way. In addition to that, it is now better and better understood that the health of humans would be improved if people ate more of the fatty acids contained in fish oils. The well-known British nutritionist Professor Hugh Sinclair, after having spent some time living with the Eskimos, came up with a simple slogan to sum up the importance of fish in the human diet: 'A herring a day keeps the doctor away.' He also showed that the unsaturated fatty acids found in fish oils have the property of reducing the permeability of the skin to water in animals living in the Arctic. It is tempting to interpret the need to consume these fatty acids as a sign of adaptation to water. Of course seafoods contain more than fatty acids alone; they also provide vitamins A and D, high-quality protein and minerals such as selenium. Sardines contain 3 mg of zinc per 100 g, and oysters 45–70 mg per 100 g. Some cultivatable algae, such as spirulina, could be a food of the future for our species. Generally speaking, it is fair to say that the optimum dietary needs of humans cannot be met without including some kind of sea products.

Eating fish every Friday, which is the traditional advice of the Catholic Church, could be seen as evidence of a profound understanding of human needs, as far as nutrition is concerned. Perhaps the roots of the extraordinary popularity of fishing as a pastime go beyond the simple need to look at water.

Our control mechanism for salt hunger is another characteristic feature of man where diet is concerned. Man's need for salt cannot be precisely specified: the salt intake of some natives of the New Guinea highlands is a small fraction of 1 g a day, while in northern Honshu, Japan, it can be 30 g a day, with a tendency towards high blood-pressure. Why do we eat four kilos of salt a year, when even the most active person needs only a quarter of this amount?

The Diseased Ape

There are some diseases that are suffered only by humans, which lends weight to the argument that we are adapted to water. For example, asthma is an extremely common disease among humans, yet it is unknown among apes. During an asthma attack there is excessive contraction of the smooth bronchial muscles. This particular mechanism is used by some sea mammals when diving to reduce their lung capacity, to make the body less buoyant and to avoid nitrogen intoxication and decompression sickness.

There are several skin disorders that occur only in humans. Examples of these are acne, seborrhoea and sebaceous cysts. These disorders are linked to an overactivity of the sebaceous glands, which are glands in the skin that secrete an oily substance called sebum. Seborrhoea is merely excessive secretion of sebum. Acne happens when the duct of the gland is blocked by a keratin plug. When the gland grows to a considerable size, for example on the scalp, it is a sebaceous cyst.

Overactivity of the sebaceous glands is so common among adolescents that it could be considered as a normal stage in the development of human skin. What is this process all about? Why have we this ability to cover our skin with a thin film of fat? Is it evidence of adaptation to water? One might add this fact to the property fish oils have to reduce the permeability of the skin to water.

Then there is the human shoulder, which is particularly vulnerable. When you are on duty in a casualty department, you learn that dislocation of the shoulder is one of the most common emergencies. Some people have only to move their arm too far backwards and upwards in order to dislocate it. This fragility of the human shoulder is the price we pay for having enormous mobility, which again is specific to humans. This mobility makes swimming easier.

In the Western world the main cause of death in the first year of life is sudden infant death, also known as cot death. One out of every 500 babies dies of cot death in Europe and North America. Cot death happens only to humans and is unknown among other animals. The typical story is when an apparently healthy baby is found dead in its cot at the end of the night. The autopsy cannot find any cause of death. Cot death is considered by some to be an inability of the baby to start breathing again after a pause. It is a kind of breathing arousal deficiency.

It is very important to note that cot death does not happen before the age of three weeks, when breathing is still completely under the control of the most primitive structures of the brain. It happens during the critical period when the baby learns to manipulate its cries voluntarily, that is when the neocortex learns to play a role in the control of the respiratory rhythm.

The specifically human breathing control mechanisms have been interpreted with reference to the human ability to dive. They also make speech possible. During the critical period when the cortical control mechanisms are developing, the sleeping baby is vulnerable. It needs the best possible environment. In particular it needs a certain amount of carbon dioxide, the physiological stimulant of breathing. The baby has receptors to carbon dioxide in its nasal mucosa. The best way for a baby to avoid a lack of carbon dioxide in the atmosphere where he sleeps is for him to share his parents' bedroom. When a baby sleeps with his mother, they exchange their expelled carbon dioxide.

Interestingly enough, cot death is exceptionally rare in Hong Kong, where the living conditions are extremely crowded and where the density of population is among the highest in the world. As Dr P. Davies wrote in the *Lancet*: 'In Hong Kong the question, "When can I put the baby into its own room?" is never raised.'

It is possible that in the foreseeable future we will have sufficient data to connect some human metabolic diseases with our adaptation to the sea. For example, some people develop premature and severe hardening of the arteries, or atherosclerosis, correlated with the absence of a factor that is essential for the regulation of blood fats. All mammals have this factor, which is called apo-protein E (or apo E), except sea-lions and harbour seals. But sea-lions and harbour seals feed exclusively on fish, and the so-called omega 3 fatty acids that are prevalent in the diet of these sea mammals create totally different metabolic conditions. Perhaps they do not need apoprotein, because their only food is fish, or maybe they have another protective factor not yet discovered.

The study of diseases can be taken together with the study of congenital abnormalities. It is well known that when a congenital abnormality takes the form of adding a feature, it usually means that this feature had a reason for being there during the evolutionary process. One of the most common abnormalities is webbing between the toes. In 1926, in a group of 1,000 schoolchildren, it was found that 90 boys and 66 girls had webbing between the second and third toes. The Agaiumba of New Guinea, who disappeared at the beginning of this century after a massacre by a neighbouring tribe, were perfectly adapted to an aquatic life. They had an epidermal growth between the toes and were commonly described as 'duck-footed'. In fact, the whole of man's foot is different from the ape's in that the big toe is joined to the others in man, but is separated from them in apes. This connection between the toes could be considered to be the equivalent of webbing. In the same way the triangle of skin that prevents us making an angle of more than 90° between the thumb and the forefinger is a feature not found in any other primate. This could also be interpreted as the equivalent of webbing.

Asthma, acne, dislocated shoulders, cot death, toe webbing – these are arguably the most common specifically human diseases or abnormalities. For each of them we found a possible link with adaptation to water.

The Birth-attending Ape

Since the idea of writing this book began by observing births, we cannot omit a comparison between the way humans, apes and dolphins are born. It is not an easy task, because every episode of human sexuality is more or less under the control of the prevailing culture. It is difficult nowadays to pick out what is specifically human in the process of birth.

When birth among humans is compared with that among apes, the most striking difference is the mechanical difficulties encountered by our species. Apes have no real pelvic cavity. The vulva is perfectly centred. The measurements of the baby's head are always smaller than the mother's skeleton. With humans, the diameter of the baby's head between the forehead and the occiput is larger than the antero-posterior diameter of the mother's pelvis. It is the same story if you measure the distance between the baby's shoulders. In order to be born, the human body has to follow a complex journey in the form of a spiral.

Most primates give birth in the intimacy of night-time, without any help. In a wild environment the mother ape usually eats the placenta and tends to swallow everything around her that is bloody. One might say that there is no basic difference between the birth of apes and that of most other terrestrial mammals.

By contrast, dolphins and other sea mammals have two distinguishing factors where birth is concerned. First, there is usually an experienced female, a midwife, ready to welcome the baby and bring it to the surface so it can take its first breath. Birth is a female event. The males protect the circle of females from a distance, ready to kill sharks, the only dangerous predators for baby dolphins. Male dolphins can kill sharks by kicking them on the side, in the liver. Second, the mother dolphin does not eat the placenta as other mammals do.

These two ways in which dolphins are special among mammals are similar to normal human behaviour. To be assisted by an experienced woman, a midwife, is the rule in many cultures. This is what history and anthropology tell us. It seems that in very primitive cultures, before the age of metal, the labouring woman used to isolate herself and often give birth without any help. It is like this in a film made among the Eipos, a tribe in New Guinea. It was apparently the same in many other cultures, such as the Canadian Indians or the Turkmens near the Caspian Sea. In cultures where women isolate themselves, deliveries are not considered to be very difficult or very painful.

Nobody knows how the hunter–gatherers were born more than 50,000 years ago, in the tropical areas. One can guess that the weather conditions and the type of housing made it possible for the woman in labour to be isolated but able to call for help if she needed it.

After having been involved in the deliveries of thousands of women coming from several different cultures and environments, I came to the conclusion that the easiest and fastest births entail isolation during the first stage and a need for help only for the birth itself. The cry that is specific to the very last contractions could be a call for help. During the first stage of labour there is always a tendency to underestimate the importance of privacy and isolation and to overestimate the need for help from other people.

There are important speculative questions to be asked about the placenta. Nobody knows if there was a stage in the history of mankind when it was common to eat the placenta. I often saw women who were still in a profound state of regression after the expulsion of the placenta: this was totally instinctive, as if they had not yet come out of their inner trip. But I never saw one of them give the slightest hint of wanting to bring the placenta to her mouth. I know of women who ate some placenta, but these were intellectuals who had read that eating the placenta is an instinct shared by every mammal, and that the placenta contains vitamins, minerals and hormones that can help the uterus retract. If human mothers never ate the placenta from instinct, perhaps this is another feature that suggests adaptation to an aquatic environment.

The Big-brained Ape

The human brain is usually considered to be the organ that gives us mastery over all forms of life on the planet. It is apparently the most complex structure we know about in the universe. Perhaps it is as complex as the universe itself. Is it too complex to be included in a triangular study of man–ape–dolphin?

It is not sacrilege to compare the human brain with the ape brain. Many people have done this. Objective studies have demonstrated differences only in size, development and complexity of the neocortex. But there are no differences in its basic nature, and no new structures have been acquired by man. One can only reach the conclusion that man has reached a degree of encephalization that makes him different from other primates.

By contrast, although whales and dolphins belong to an order of mammals very distant from the primates, they share with man a huge cerebral development, which is apparently of the same scale. One could even put forward the claim that the degree of encephalization of the dolphin is greater than that of man, if you just compare weight and size. It is worth noting that 95.9 per cent of the human brain is covered by the neocortex, whereas it covers 97.8 per cent of the dolphin's brain.

However, things are not quite so straightforward. First, 20 per cent of the dolphin's brain is composed of the cerebellum, which controls the co-ordination of movements. Certainly it is not by chance that dolphins are so graceful and so perfectly co-ordinated. Second, in order to assess the degree of encephalization, one has to take into account the number of layers of cells in the cortex, the density of cells, the amount of folds on the surface, and the degree of specialization of the different regions. As soon as all these factors are taken into consideration, comparisons become difficult and any interpretation contradictory. The differentiation of the cell layers is less precise than in man. The density of cells is lower, but the total surface area is far greater because of the complexity and great number of folds. In total, the number of neocortical cells would be about the same in both dolphin and man, but in dolphins the cells are more widely spread.

The point of these comparisons is to contrast the intelligence of man with that of the dolphin. But this evaluation takes account of only one form of intelligence – the specifically human one. And this discussion could take us further away from a deep understanding about the behaviour of cetaceans. Perhaps they have a type of intelligence that is impossible for us to measure by our own criteria. Because we cannot imagine forms of intelligence other than our own, we concentrate all our curiosity on the neocortex as a cybernetic machine, a computer. These thoughts prompted me to focus my curiosity on some characteristics of the dolphin's brain that are often overlooked.

One of the outstanding characteristics of the dolphin's brain can be found under the cortex. It concerns the thalamus. *Thalamus* is a Greek word meaning 'chamber'. The thalamus is what the hemispheres of the brain lie in. All information, including painful stimulation, arrives at the thalamus first, before reaching the cortex. All sensory functions, with the exception of the sense of smell, are relayed in the thalamus. The most striking thing about the dolphin's thalamus is the extensive expansion of something called intrinsic nuclei. These are groups of cells that do not receive any stimulus from outside the thalamus. These nuclei project upon zones of the neocortex that are situated between the main sensory zones. In order to cover up our relative ignorance of the significance of these zones, they are called 'silent' or 'associative' zones. I made a connection between the exceptional development of the intrinsic thalamic nuclei and the very small proportion of the cortex devoted to sensory projection. Myron

Jacobs and Peter Morgan have shown that much more than 90 per cent of the dolphin's cortex can be considered as silent or associative. The figures are 90 per cent in man, 75 per cent in apes, 50 per cent in cats and 10 per cent in rabbits.

At one end of the scale of mammals is the brain of an animal like the rabbit, which can do no more than analyse information given to it by the sensory organs. At the other end of the scale are the brains of man and the dolphin, which are capable of activities not directly triggered by the sensory brain.

However, one should not underestimate the extraordinary development of the sensory functions of dolphins. Everyone has heard about the quality of their hearing and their abilities in echolocation. It is less common to mention the acuteness of their vision, but a dolphin is able to snatch a sardine from a trainer's mouth when he is standing on a board twenty-five feet above the water's surface. Dolphins are excellent at seeing things at a distance under water, at seeing things near by while in the air, and at seeing through the surface of the water. It is thought that dolphins can see in colour; they have cells in the retina that appear to be the equivalent of cones. Dolphins can also move each of their eyes independently from the other, so they can look in front of them with one eye while at the same time looking behind them with the other one!

Dolphins have very sensitive skin, so they spend a lot of their time rubbing and caressing each other. Even if they have no sense of smell, their sense of taste is extremely well developed. They can locate each other from great distances and find schools of fish thanks to their ability to taste traces of urine and faeces in parts per billion.

It has been calculated that the dolphin can receive at least ten times more information through its sense organs than we can. But the dolphin does not have hands, and the hand can be considered a true sensory organ, with its immense zone of projection on the brain.

Despite all this, the greatest part of the cortex in the dolphin, just as in man, *has much more to do* than simply to analyse the information given to it by the sensory organs. It is as if, set free from practical worries, humans and dolphins have time to think. In other words, we have an inkling of what the physiological basis of abstract thinking might be, and even of spirituality. Such speculations as these, based on anatomical data, can be added to the comments made by John Lilly after observing the behaviour of dolphins. He thinks that dolphins and whales naturally veer towards directions one can call spiritual. They can reach meditative states very simply and very easily. But what does the dolphin do with its intelligence? This is the first question that springs to mind when you are aware of the extraordinary development of its brain. What does this animal, which is at the end of the food chain and is even able to kill sharks, do with its intelligence?

To answer this question, it must be assumed that the dolphin's intelligence is totally different from ours, which is entirely oriented towards the domination of other species, at the risk of destroying the whole planet in the process. What can an animal do with its intelligence if not 'born with the psychology of world conquest' – the trait that Montessori could detect in the baby as soon as he feels an urge or need to face the outer world and 'absorb' it?

What makes the human brain unique? Its most characteristic feature is probably the hugely developed anterior part, or prefrontal cortex; it is recognized that this plays a role in relating past, present and future, and making anticipation possible.

A comparative study of the brains of man and dolphin would be a fruitful area of research; no one has even scratched its surface. For example, we know nothing about the number of glial cells in the dolphin's brain. In fact, we know very little about the role of these cells at all. What we do know is that in the lower-left parietal lobe of Einstein's brain there was a high ratio of glial cells to neurons. But what about the dolphin's brain?

The most promising path for research will probably take into account a difference in the way the brains work: men dream; dolphins apparently do not. Unlike most of the other mammals, dolphins do not have a phase of 'rapid eye movement' sleep, which might dramatically increase the efficiency of the brain by putting in order our memorized facts. So, with an equivalent degree of encephalization, the dolphin can be less 'intelligent' than man. The point is to explain why, with such a developed cortex, dolphins are not able to resolve simple, practical problems such as how to get away from the nets of the tuna-fishers.

Although our knowledge of the dolphin's brain (and indeed man's brain) is still rudimentary, one can nevertheless conclude that the degree of encephalization is comparable in the two species. Here again a feature that makes us different from the other primates tends to bring us closer to the sea mammals.

These considerations bring us back to a rule which had been established by Konrad Lorenz: the box that encases the brain – and therefore the brain itself – is bigger in sea mammals than in their terrestrial cousins. It is bigger, for example, in the otter than in the stoat. The swimming monkey of Gabon, the talapoin, is sometimes called the 'Buddhist monk' because its brain case is very large in comparison with its body weight. Professor Michael Crawford at the Institute of Zoology in London explained that this is due to a marine diet. The sea contains a large amount of vitamins, minerals and other nutrients that facilitate brain development. Other explanations do not contradict this. When a mammal is swimming under water, the carbon dioxide levels in its bloodstream increase. This might be a way to develop and maintain the expansion of the carotid arteries and to improve the vascularization of the brain. Carbon dioxide therapy has been used with brain-damaged children.

*

Our triangular study of man–ape–dolphin carries with it the conviction that the aquatic capacities of man are still unknown or at least underestimated. Of course, we cannot reach a conclusion about our degree of adaptation to water just by looking at one or two features we have in common with sea mammals. It would be easy to argue, for example, that monkeys also have some fat under the skin and that it is just a question of how much. It is also possible to claim that a parrot can have articulate language without being a diver. But what is really striking is the great number of characteristics we have in common with sea mammals and that make man an exception among the apes.

When I put together my own observations of human behaviour –

particularly during events involving deep regression such as birth – with the conclusions of this triangular study, I find myself perplexed. How has it been possible, for so many thousands of years, that countless philosophers and scholars, who were pronouncing on human nature, did so without seeing that *Homo sapiens* is above all *Homo aquaticus*? Until now, hardly anyone has looked at the dolphin in order to better understand man.

CHAPTER 8
Homo Aquaticus

The Missing Link

The theories put forward by fossil hunters illustrate how specialization can sometimes narrow the horizon. These specialists apparently know nothing about the theories of Alister Hardy, which advance the idea that man might be descended from an aquatic primate. Why do they never mention this theory, or at least explain their reasons for dismissing it? The few palaeo-anthropologists who mentioned the aquatic theory preferred to avoid any serious analysis and just wrote some dismissive sentences about it. Glynn Isaac, for example, considered the aquatic hypothesis highly implausible or impossible' but added 'it is fun to keep it on the list in the meanwhile'. J. Gowlett considered it 'only slightly less far-fetched than Erich von Daniken's extra-terrestrials'.

In attempting to take stock of the current theories about human evolution, one must never forget that 'the field has had more than its quota of temperament problems'. An eminent palaeontologist summarized this phenomenon in a subtle and elegant way: 'What we pick as essential human attributes, and how we trace their development, often tell us as much about palaeoanthropologists and the time in which they live as about the course of evolutionary events.' One day somebody should write a thesis about the personality of the fossil hunters. It would be fruitful to put together all the various strange stories about them. For example, there is a story about how Eugène Dubois found the remains of the Java man in the 1890s but kept them underneath his floor until 1926! Or there is the story of the Peking man. It started in 1921 with the discovery by O. Zdansky of teeth that were the first fossil evidence of hominids in China. Zdansky decided to keep quiet about his findings, not even telling his companions, and then chose to reveal the discovery five years later for the Crown Prince and Princess of Sweden during a state visit to China. There is the story of Raymond Dart, who discovered in 1924 an infant's skull that was obviously odd in a number of respects. Dart called his find Australopithecus. It was not until 1934 that some authoritative palaeontologists were obliged to give importance to this breakthrough.

There is also food for thought in the behaviour of the famous Louis Leakey, whose interpretations of all fossil hominid finds were altered by a life-long preference for an extended *Homo sapiens* ancestry. Would the conclusion of such a thesis support the opinion of Graham Richards: 'Though you don't have to be mad to be a fossil hunter, it probably helps'?

The theory put forward in such a discreet way by Alister Hardy (see p. 57) goes with a deep knowledge of human anatomy, physiology and behaviour; he also possesses a profound knowledge of terrestrial and aquatic zoology, and of the history of seas and continents. It does not mean that the evidence provided by fossils is ignored. Indeed, some enthusiastic advocates of an aquatic phase in human evolution, such as Marc Verghaegen and Leon La Lumière, have a good knowledge of fossils. But why was it that Elaine Morgan, a writer, had to take the initiative in revealing this theory (see p. 57)?

All the other theories about the origin of our species have reached an impasse: they have been turned upside down by new information.

Until recently it was an accepted fact among fossil specialists that the human line detached itself from the other primates very early, about fifteen million years ago. The chimpanzee, gorilla and orang-utan were supposed to be very close to each other. Ramapithecus, whose fossils were found mostly in Eurasia, was considered to be the first hominid.

During the last two decades scientists have developed new methods of dating the rocks, using the transformation of radioactive potassium into an inert gas called argon. There have also been improvements in the observation of chromosomes and in the analysis of biochemical features such as blood groups, nucleic acids and proteins. By examining the amino acids that make up proteins, one can assess at which period there was a divergence between different animal species. In other words, it is possible to assess the extent of family relationships on an evolutionary scale. With these methods one can claim, for example, that a man and a chimpanzee have roughly the same degree of family relationship as a horse to a zebra, but are closer together than a dog and a fox. Even if these methods are not very precise, they are still accurate enough to establish that the orang-utan and Ramapithecus are on the same branch that diverged from the common trunk ten to fifteen million years ago.

The emergence of the human branch is probably more recent than previously believed: not more than six or seven million years ago. The discovery of the skeleton of the famous 'Lucy' and other Australopithecus from Hadar and Laetolil does nothing to help us understand when man separated from the great apes, the gorilla, and, above all, the chimpanzee. These Australopithecus are about three to four million years old. According to some experts, such as Dr Leakey, they do not belong to the branch that leads to *Homo sapiens*. In fact, the most primitive form of man that has been identified with any certainty is probably *Homo habilis* in the Olduvai Gorge, Tanzania. Its age is estimated to be 1.8 million years, a figure reached with some precision through the potassium–argon method of dating tools.

The point is that even with the current technological advances, fossil specialists cannot build one single satisfactory theory of the genesis of man. There is a blank of several million years to fill.

The Deluge

At the time of this blank period the shape of East Africa was very different from what it is today. During a period that probably started five to seven million years ago, a part of what is now Ethiopia was very likely covered by sea. This area is situated near the Red Sea, north-west of Djibouti. It corresponds to the Danakil

Alps, that is to say, the central and northern zones of the Afar triangle.

So, as La Lumière believes, the Danakil Alps might have been an island off the African continent. A great number of terrestrial animals must have died when their usual territory was flooded. But some advanced primates, the ancestors of *Homo sapiens*, might have survived by adapting to an aquatic environment. It is possible that a period of between one and a half and three million years passed before *Homo aquaticus* could go back to life on the continent after the land had dried out.

During that aquatic period our ancestor, who had lost his forests, could find both food and refuge from predators in the water. He had to be able to walk in shallow water, to swim and to dive. It is here that our ancestor might have learned to stand upright, and his hands might have become more sensitive by searching for seashells without always being able to see them. It is in such a context that man might have emerged.

Darwin knew that life on islands tends to accelerate the process of evolution. It was in the Galapagos Islands of the Pacific that he collected much of the information that supports his theory about the origin of species.

I believe there is a connection between the deluge in Ethiopia, which probably destroyed many plants and animal species, and the different variants of the deluge legend. In the Bible the deluge was a great flood that covered the earth at the time of Noah. Every living creature was destroyed except for those preserved in the ark. The other well-known deluge legend is found in the epic of Gilgamesh, a long Akkadian poem composed about 2,000 BC on the theme of human beings' futile quest for immortality. Unable to accept the finality of death, Gilgamesh goes to Utna-pishtim, the Babylonian counterpart of the biblical Noah. Utna-pishtim explains that he received the secret of his immortality because of the unique circumstances of the flood. He tells Gilgamesh of a thorny plant growing in Apsu, the sweet waters underneath the earth, that gives eternal life. Gilgamesh dives to the bottom of the waters and secures the plant, but, as he journeys home, a snake eats the plant; thus, snakes, not human beings, have eternal life. I found this legend inspiring in so far as the most primitive structures of the human brain, the so-called reptilian ones, reach their maturity during the time in the amniotic fluid. Is the reptilian brain the support of the religious sense, a vision of the universe that transcends space and time?

These two well-known legends of deluge were variants of the same basic tale known in different parts of the world. The origins of these stories are mysterious, because there is no evidence of a flood during the historical period. Could these legends be the traces, in our collective memory, of a cataclysmic event without which man would not be what he is?

More generally speaking, almost all the creation myths contain the idea of a rupture, an occurrence that separates the primordial condition from the final one. Creation often emerges from a metamorphosis from water. In many creation myths an earth diver plunges into the depths of water, bringing up a small amount of earth. In these myths water appears as the primordial matter of creation, although beneath the waters there is earth. Myths of this kind are prominent in American Indian mythology, especially among the Huron.

Still in the field of myths, it is tempting also to make connections with the Sumerian, Babylonian and Mesopotamian legends, in which civilization started with whales. Whales were supposed to have taught humans the concept of recurrent cycles as a fundamental law of nature. This might help solve an etymological mystery: why does a word that means 'cycle' (wheel) have the same root as the word 'whale' in several languages, including English and the various Scandinavian languages?

The belief that water was the beginning of all things persisted in the teaching of Thales of Miletus, whose philosophy marks the transition in Western thought from mythical forms to scientific speculations about the origins of the world.

The probability that the sea covered a part of East Africa for a period might be a key for comprehending the emergence of man; it may also be a root of cross-cultural myths and legends. It adds support to the growing conviction among evolutionists that the emergence of man was accomplished more rapidly than was once imagined. It adds powerful support to the theories of Alister Hardy. And it makes us think twice about the limitations of an approach that is based exclusively on fossils. What is the future of human corpses immersed in sea water? What are the chances of finding fossils that can be used by scientists? This difficulty is not insurmountable. Some whales are known only by their fossils. La Lumière noticed that most hominid remains have been found in rocks that seem to have been formed in lakes and estuaries.

Was Humanity Born in the Water?

We have seen that most of the features that distinguish man from the apes can be interpreted as signs of adaptation to an aquatic environment. We have drawn attention to the fact that the missing link probably corresponds to the time when part of the African continent was covered by sea. But there is still one stage to be considered before the aquatic theory can be accepted as a serious basis for reflection and study. This stage is a toing and froing between land and sea, which is a well-known and common phenomenon in the process of evolution.

Going back to the sea is an ordinary evolutionary process, involving birds such as penguins and reptiles such as crocodiles and snakes. When one thinks of the mammals who returned to the sea, cetaceans such as whales, dolphins and porpoises come first to mind. Like all mammals, they are warm-blooded animals; they breathe air, develop in the uterus before birth, and go through a period of breast-feeding. It is generally agreed that these mammals started to go back to the sea about seventy million years ago, and that they derive from two or three different terrestrial species.

It is important to realize that every known order of mammal has cousins in the water. The dugong and the manatee are the descendants of vegetarian hoofed animals; seals, sea-lions and walruses are the descendants of carnivorous animals; beavers are the cousins of purely terrestrial rodents. So why is it impossible that a primate temporarily followed the same route? This primate is man.

Man is probably not the first primate to follow this pattern.

The skeleton of an extinct variety of aquatic primate, the Oreopithecus, has been found in Italy. The bones were preserved because they sank into the mud. This primate, adapted to life in the swamp, had many points in common with man, such as the short, broad pelvis and the elbow of an upright walker, as well as a flattened face.

Since the passage between sea and land is possible in both directions, and since some animal species are amphibious, there is no *a priori* reason why certain mammals that adapted to water should not go back to dry land. This might have been so in the case of the elephant. The elephant has many things in common with aquatic mammals. It has practically no hair and has webbing between its toes. In the female, the vulva is so far to the front that it was once believed that elephants copulated face to face. The elephant's penis, like the whale's, retracts completely into a special pocket in the body wall. The opening in the skin for nostrils is above the eyes, as in sea mammals (in the elephant this is hidden because the air canal continues down inside the trunk). The elephant is an excellent swimmer and expresses emotions by shedding tears. At the birth of the baby elephant, there is always an 'aunt': an experienced female that plays the role of the midwife. The presence of a midwife might be a point in common between sea mammals, elephants and humans.

I have attempted to go beyond the things that are well known by trying to find out if the elephant's brain has something special about it. Certainly, the neocortex of the elephant is not as developed as the dolphin's (see p. 78). But the thalamus, the structure upon which the brain hemispheres lie, has many points in common in both species. The intrinsic nuclei, the nerve cells that do not receive any stimulation from outside and that project on to the cortex between the sensory areas, are particularly well developed. Is this common point of dolphins and humans a sign of adaptation to water? Or is this feature particular only to those animals that have nothing to fear from predators and who are also freed from some practical considerations?

The Irrational Basis of a Theory

One can claim that the rational and objective bases of the aquatic theories are solid. But when the object of one's study is the genesis of our species, our own history, ourselves, we have to go beyond any rational basis. We have to make use of the irrational side of ourselves to reinforce, or weaken, our acceptance of a theory. Theories take on a greater value and interest if they are seductive, attractive, fascinating, and if it is easy to stick to them by an act of faith before carefully analysing their rational basis. Glynn Isaac confessed in his book about human evolution: 'Our new origin beliefs are, in fact, surrogate myths, that are themselves part science, part myth ... People clearly want to be free to choose their evolutionary origin stories. Bear this in mind as you read this and other accounts of human evolution.'

During his development, a human being has to reproduce, or rather summarize, the process of evolution, particularly at the stage in the womb. It is as if the history of life was imprinted on a kind of memory. Our irrational behaviour gives credence to the existence of this sort of memory. For example, all mammals are frightened of snakes. Probably at some remote stage in our evolution there was a merciless fight between mammals and reptiles. One can suppress this fear of snakes in primates by destroying a very precise area of the primitive part of the brain, where this fear is supposed to be imprinted.

The theory of the aquatic ape is indeed a very attractive one. Apparently this is something that Alister Hardy had not at first foreseen and did not take into consideration later. He presented his hypothesis for the first time at the British Sub-Aqua Club in Brighton and afterwards wrote: 'I did not expect the wide publicity that was given to my views in the daily press.' One can imagine that journalists, who tend to reflect the reactions of the general public, could have strongly supported the preliminary hypothesis. But Hardy chose not to pursue this theory and preferred to dedicate himself to research involving features of human nature that he felt to be even more important than man's aquatic past.

I was faced with the same kind of dilemma before putting together all the observations, information and thoughts that make up this book. But it was precisely because of the attitude of journalists and the general public that I realized how important this topic was. I now have a different vision of the human being. Such an accord, such a harmony, between the objective and subjective points of view is a preview of a radically new era in our understanding of the human phenomenon.

A period of transition is gradually beginning to happen. We are witnessing a new stage in the relationship between humans and the sea, and between humans and sea mammals, symbolized by dolphins. The popularity throughout the world of someone like Jacques Cousteau, the success of TV films such as *Flipper*, the creation of centres for studying dolphins, the interest in birth under water, are all symptoms of the dawning of this new understanding of the human phenomenon. The new era does not need well-established theories in order to take root, but a strong theoretical basis will give it a powerful push upwards.

The Beginning of a Conspiracy

Humans have always collaborated with animals. Sheepdogs, watchdogs, horses, mules, reindeers, carrier-pigeons, are all well-known examples of animals who are at the service of man. There are Greek legends about dolphins saving humans, as well as many other stories of sea mammals working with humans. The US Navy used trained dolphins in the Gulf of Suez to locate mines. There is also the story of three seals called Stanley, Razz and Sirius; they were trained to perform rescue operations considered too difficult for human divers. But until now there has been no regular collaboration that benefits both man and dolphins. One of the main exceptions to this has been the way that fishermen traditionally work together with dolphins in Mauritania. The fish are rounded up partly by the dolphins and partly by the humans. In a place such as this, killing a dolphin is tantamount to killing a man.

When Tcharkovsky gave some pregnant women the chance to swim with dolphins in the Black Sea, he opened up a new era in inter-species collaboration. According to Tcharkovsky, it is as if the stomach of a pregnant woman is transparent to the sonar system of dolphins. He believes that dolphins can establish real communication with a human foetus, to the extent of being able to pass on some of their knowledge and to teach them not to be afraid of water. It appears that female dolphins are particularly interested in pregnant women, and it has been claimed that they would even be able to bring the new-born baby to the surface in an underwater birth. Many people will be sceptical about this. It is difficult to know how much fantasy plays a part in human births attended by dolphin midwives. Our need for legends goes together with our need for irrationality. But perhaps one day, thanks to pioneers like Tcharkovsky, we will be better able to answer the question: what can dolphins do with their intelligence?

We should not forget that in past ages humans were born near animals. Christ was born in a stable. I personally have been very interested by the attitude of cats during human births. They seem to understand what's happening, but one hardly notices them. Their behaviour might be used as a model by midwives. These stories of dolphins attending human births have inspired therapeutic aquatic projects, where dolphins would be involved.

The therapeutic power of animals is certainly well known. The companionship of animals has always been considered as meeting a fundamental human need, a necessary condition for maintaining well-being. The Egyptians revered cats; the Phoenicians used to travel with their cats and dogs; the Romans domesticated polecats. Modern scientific research has shown that stroking an animal slows down the heart rate and lowers the blood pressure. A study compared two groups of elderly people. One group was given budgerigars and the other houseplants. The people in the first group had a tendency to make more friends, to live longer, and to keep their capacity for speech. At a meeting of the World Veterinary Association in Montreal it was argued that it was unnatural *not* to keep pets.

If you are aware of the therapeutic power of water, if you are aware of the therapeutic effect of the companionship given by animals, and if you are aware of the special relationship between humans and dolphins, you are more likely to take seriously certain projects for therapeutic aquatic centres, where swimming with dolphins would be possible.

At the Dolphins Plus Center in Key Largo, Florida, they are beyond the stage of just making plans. The Borguss Family, who have extensive experience in caring for animals in zoos and training animals for the circus, owned six dolphins that had been trained for shows. The Borguss family decided to try a different approach and put their dolphins in a deep, man-made cove in a canal. From there the dolphins could return to the ocean when they wanted to, but were protected from sharks by a special barrier. This centre became a place where people could come and swim with the dolphins.

Soon after the Borguss family brought their dolphins to Key Largo, they were joined by Betsy Smith, a specialist in autistic children at the University of Florida. Autistic teenagers can now come into contact with the dolphins on a daily basis, either staying on a platform where the dolphins can be playful with them or entering the water itself. The first observations were promising: dolphins seem to have the ability to push autistic children to communicate.

While ordinary domestic animals like dogs and cats don't bother to make an effort when someone is unresponsive to them, dolphins never give up. They always stay friendly, full of fun, and even joyful. The Dolphins Plus Center has also opened its doors to the terminally ill, paraplegics, quadraplegics, amputees, and a group of blind, and deaf and blind, teenagers. With people who cannot cope with the loss of a familiar person, the contact with dolphins can have a deeply positive effect, the more so since it is coming from something other than a human form.

The experience of the Dolphins Plus Center confirms the powerful mutual attraction between humans and dolphins. Dolphins are particularly interested in humans; people have always been mystified and fascinated by dolphins. This attraction can even be sexual. There are strange stories of inter-species love-affairs . . . The least confidential one is a relationship between the Frenchman François Xavier Pelletier and Koutta, a young female freshwater dolphin, a *Platanista gangetica* (Ganges dolphin), in a swimming-pool in Dacca. Pelletier tells this story in detail in his *Ballade pour un dauphin sacré*.

Some people are convinced that dolphins – in a way difficult to imagine – will help us protect the planet against destruction.

There are those who believe they have received messages from dolphins. In the name of dolphins, they dare tell us some home truths about ourselves. Could we be going towards a man–dolphin conspiracy?

Communication between humans and dolphins should not be thought of as a new phenomenon. For thousands of years the remote aborigines of the Gulf of Carpentaria in northern Australia have claimed that they were in direct communication with wild dolphins. Their shamans were supposed to speak with the dolphins 'mind to mind' using a complex series of whistles.

There are architects of underwater life, such as Jacques Rougerie, the author of *Aquaspace*, or artists who specialize in the relationship between man and dolphin, such as Louis Girault, Scott Thorn and Jean-Luc Bozzoli. What these men have in common is that they look to the future: their primary concern is the fate of the planet. It is significant that both Cousteau and Tcharkovsky, who know our aquatic abilities better than anybody, talk about the human being as a mammal who might return to the sea. They see a link between our potential and our future, and don't waste any time analysing the past.

While giving lectures, I have sometimes talked about the aquatic theories of the origins of man. This theory always immediately attracts a certain type of person – young, enthusiastic, ready to build a new era. When you are endowed with a human consciousness, an interest in the future is an aspect of sexuality: only humans can express their sexual nature through a vision of the future that goes beyond their own death.

CHAPTER 9
Homo demens

Above the entrance
Of the oracle of its namesake, Delphi,
Was written the salutary phrase *Gnothi seauton*
Know thyself

– Heathcote Williams, *Falling for a Dolphin*

Has *Homo aquaticus* become *Homo demens*? The behaviour typified by the current representatives of man is difficult to study, because it arouses our collective sense of guilt. Is it even possible to look our own dementia in the face? Some people will be inclined to find the topic boring and avoid it. But evasion is no longer permissible and the precept 'know thyself' now applies to humanity as a whole.

Let us recall some well-known facts to evaluate the degree of our dementia.

The Cycle of Water

Turn on the tap, and you are in touch with a phenomenon that has no beginning and no end. It is the cycle of water.

One way or another the tap water will go to the river, and from the river to the sea. Evaporation from the seas will make clouds, which will return water to the earth's surface in the form of rain. Rain-water will infiltrate the earth and create ground water, including underground streams. It is thanks to the ground water that we can turn on the tap . . .

Man, who owes everything to water, has become a monstrous saboteur of its natural cycle. The destruction of the earth's forests is one aspect of this gross interference. These areas have the capacity to maintain huge quantities of water. Their destruction leads to aridity and drought in a process that is commonly called 'desertification'. Forty per cent of the rain forests have already disappeared, and the process continues at a dizzy speed – in the region of eight million acres a year over the whole planet. Africa is the continent most affected, losing about five million acres annually. During the last thirty years, Central America has lost two thirds of its forests.

'When trees go, deserts come.' Deserts are created by man. By disturbing the cycle of water, man is destroying life. *One cannot understand human nature without studying the process of desertification.* Indeed, the phenomenon is not new. The felling of the cedars of Lebanon had begun as early as 3000 BC, after which they formed the cornerstone of the Phoenicians' international trade. The Pharaohs imported forty ship loads of cedar. After that the temples and palaces of Assyria and Babylon were built of cedar coming from a subjugated Lebanon. King Solomon built his temple in Jerusalem in the same fashion. Not until the Roman emperor Hadrian in the second century BC was any attempt made to protect the remaining trees. In ancient Greece, Plato commented on the destruction of forests: 'Our land, compared with what it was, is like the skeleton of a body wasted by disease.' A large part of northern Africa, which was once the 'granary of Rome', is now desert. In 1620 New England in North America was entirely forested, but almost completely deforested 150 years later. Arkansas saw its many acres of marsh and swamp forest converted to farms.

The process of deforestation can be justified only by short-term benefits and an inability to break a vicious circle. Felling trees makes agriculture and cattle-breeding possible for the time being. But soon the water table may start to fall, the area becomes arid . . . and more trees have to be cut down.

Half of the wood used in the world is burned, either directly or as charcoal. The average citizen in a Third World country burns as much wood every year as a North American consumes in the form of paper. Where trees are scarce, people are forced to collect the dung dropped by livestock for use as fuel. In India sixty million tons of dried dung are burned as fuel each year, providing 10 per cent of the country's energy. The main consequence is the soil's infertility. This is the vicious circle from which the Third World cannot escape.

One commonly underestimates how diverse and serious are the effects of interference in the cycle of water. These effects can be felt thousands of miles away: for example, the flow of rivers can be upset. When the trees in the Himalayas are felled, the monsoon rains are not contained and areas in India and Bangladesh are either flooded or dried up. Over a period of some decades, the destruction of the rain forests has caused the extinction of many animal and plant species that had developed over millions and millions of years. It has been calculated that four square miles of typical tropical forests can shelter 1,500 species of flowering plants, 750 trees, 400 birds, 150 butterflies, 125 mammals, 100 reptiles and 50 amphibians. Furthermore, 3,000 plants known to have anti-cancer properties are in danger of extinction, according to the US National Cancer Institute. As for the effects on the climate, these are still difficult to evaluate, but they might be perceptible as soon as the twenty-first century begins.

The consequences of deforestation on the cycle of water raise problems beyond frontiers. That is why it is so difficult to solve them, although it is theoretically possible. There is a constant conflict between local and short-term considerations and the long-term interests of the planet as a whole.

Take, for example, the attitude of the American authorities. In December 1985 Congress passed a law preventing the development banks from supporting or assisting projects that could damage the rain forests. As a result, a loan of several million dollars to Brazil was vetoed because the money would have paid for the destruction of Amazonian forests. Thanks to this legislation some nations in the Third World have understood the benefits of looking after their rain forests ... But one country that has not stopped destroying its rain forests is the United States itself. These forests are mostly in Hawaii; others in Puerto Rico and on some Pacific islands are also under American control. In Hawaii, although deforestation began 1,500 years ago with the arrival of the Polynesians, half the island's land surface was still covered with forests 200 years ago, when the Europeans and Americans came. They now cover a mere 5 per cent, and the destruction continues. There are short-term advantages in converting forest to pasture for cattle. Wood can be sold to the Hawaii Electric Light Company, and owners of these areas pay lower taxes. But it should not be forgotten that zoologists find Hawaii at least as interesting as Darwin found the Galapagos Islands. Of its animals and plants, 95 per cent are unique, specific to the place! Most of them are either extinct or in grave danger.

Using wood as fuel destroys the forests, but it also disrupts the cycle of water in other ways. The extensive use of combustible materials, whatever their origins, as sources of energy tends to change the ratio between water and carbon dioxide in the atmosphere. It tends to exaggerate the 'greenhouse effect'; in other words, it tends to raise the mean temperature of the earth's surface. One can see how the cycle of water is disturbed, in that warm air contains more water vapour than cooler air. It is expected that the distribution of rainfall, as well as sea levels, will be affected in the future.

Acid Rain

Man not only disturbs the cycle of water, he also pollutes the rain. This phenomenon has been brought to the public attention by the phrase 'acid rain'.

The first effects of the chemical pollution of water were evident in Scandinavian countries, when they discovered the acidity of their lakes and rivers. Early symptoms were that many fish and other aquatic species died. But international awareness was awakened when the German forests were affected. The first alarms were raised in the 1970s in southern Germany, when the needles of the silver firs turned yellow and dropped off. By 1984, 50 per cent of forests in Germany were affected to some degree, although few trees actually died. The first interpretations were simple, in particular near the borders with Poland and Czech-oslovakia, where the levels of sulphur dioxide and nitrogen oxides were high enough to affect the trees directly. But in the Black Forest and elsewhere, such as Los Angeles and the surrounding area, they needed other explanations and had to take into account the ozone layer and the prevailing levels of hydrocarbons.

The main sources of pollution of rain-water are power stations, factories and cars. The progression of this kind of pollution has been studied by an ingenious method in Greenland, in a place where there is no local pollution. They drilled out a column of ice from a glacier. By studying the extent to which radioactive oxygen in the core had decayed, they were able to tell the age of the ice at different depths. This revealed an accurate picture of pollution levels over the previous 115 years. They pointed out that since 1870 global emissions of man-made sulphur had increased 25-fold, and that nitrate levels had doubled since 1975.

The Water Desert

Human beings express their lack of concern for the future of life on the planet by creating deserts both on land and in the water. 'Dying waters' is now a well-accepted concept where rivers, lakes and inland seas such as the Mediterranean and the Adriatic are concerned. All the seas and oceans are threatened by irreversible imbalances.

In the Gulf of Mexico, 3,000 square miles of low-oxygen water have been found. In the western portion of Long Island Sound, the lack of oxygen explains widespread fish deaths. In Chesapeake Bay thousands of fish, crabs and oysters have died in places where high levels of sulphide have been reported. Similar danger signals have been raised up and down the east coast of North America, notably the deaths of over 200 dolphins washed ashore from New Jersey to Virginia.

At the opening of the North Sea Environment Ministers' Conference, Prince Charles said that the North Sea had been turned into a vast rubbish dump, full of effluents that threaten its ecological balance. He added: 'The North Sea is not a bottomless pit of our waste and it makes no sense to test it to destruction.' Pollutants derived from agricultural fertilizers and sewage probably caused the disastrous outbreak of the 'killer algae', known as Danish algae in Sweden and as Swedish algae in Denmark. In three weeks 500 tonnes of salmon were killed.

The history of whale hunting can be used to illustrate the behaviour of humans towards marine creatures, as well as life in general. It is just another story of desertification.

The first records of a commercial approach to whaling can be found in the Basque country between France and Spain and date from about AD 900. The sailors used to pursue the Biscayan right whales with small boats. These whales swam slowly and floated when dead. It was possible to follow them until they were exhausted, then to kill them with harpoons and tow them to the shore. The whale oil was used mostly in lamps. When the Basque whalers had completely exterminated this species around the sixteenth century, they had to go up to Iceland and Greenland to hunt another right whale, the bow-head. They were joined by the English and Dutch. The bow-heads were commercially extinct within fifty years.

The beginning of the eighteenth century was the great period for the American whalers who killed 200,000 right whales before being obliged to go further offshore; that is how they came to start hunting the sperm whales. This reached a peak in the middle of the nineteenth century, and the stocks of sperm whale in the Atlantic were exhausted by the 1920s. During the eighteenth century other American whalers concentrated on the western side of the Arctic. These Pacific whalers were often idle during the winter months, until in 1853 Captain Charles Scammon discovered the calving grounds of the grey whales in Baja, California, so the whalers could be active even in winter. They introduced a new technique of first harpooning the young calf to attract its mother. This continued for about fifty years, until the species was threatened with extinction. Now, thanks to measures taken by the Mexican government, the species will survive and the population of grey whales is estimated to be about 18,000. The last species to be depleted were the blue, the fin and the sei in the Antarctic. The minkes are now the mainstay of the Antarctic whalers – but they are not worth the trouble of catching . . .

Whaling is a global problem and, as with man's interference with the cycle of water, national frontiers should be disregarded. Both cases demonstrate the consequences of unresolved conflicts between local and short-term interests on the one hand, and global and long-term interests on the other. Indeed, there is an international whaling commission that has banned the hunt for sperm whales in the waters of the north-west Pacific, off the coast of Japan, and established quotas elsewhere. But whaling states and nations protest, or resign their membership of the commission, or just go on hunting the whales. The last loophole that has been exploited is whaling 'for the purposes of scientific research'.

We call *Homo demens* the man who is unable to avoid the collective urge for destruction created by such unresolved conflicts. Has man an innately destructive instinct? Is this instinct the original sin? How will the planet, considered as a living being, react to the activity of man as a parasitic species? Perhaps the earth will just reach another equilibrium, another homeostasis incompatible with the survival of our species, in the same way that we get rid of the flu virus by changing our homeostasis and raising our temperature.

The time has come to study man as an agent of desertification. This angle of human nature needs the utmost attention. We cannot conceive of anything with greater priority.

Is it the emotional desert in man that creates the desert in nature? Should modern education first make the technological man able to see far into the future? Where a vision of the future is concerned, we are genetically as short-sighted as the hunter–gatherer. But the actions of prehistoric man had only short-term consequences, if the entire history of the planet is taken into account.

CHAPTER 10

Outline of a Theory of Emotion-instincts

Emotional desert ... release of emotions ... release of instincts ... religious instinct ... The power of water on humans prompts us to use words that many people avoid. Some scientists eschew the word 'emotion' because they cannot give it a precise definition. As for the word 'instinct', it is good form in certain circles to claim that it does not apply to human beings.

Where genital sexuality is concerned, or in the case of childbirth or therapy, we have found that water has the power to release inhibitions. This gives rise to two questions: what is inhibited? And by what is it inhibited? A modern redefinition of emotions and instincts goes hand in hand with the answer to these questions.

Barriers that Get in the Way

There are two aspects of mankind that philosophers have described in different ways throughout the ages, and that can be referred to in modern scientific terms. These two faces of man are the very reason for philosophy: heart and reason. Reason and passion. Logic and intuition. Intellect and sensitivity ...

Man has two brains. These can work together, but they can also be in conflict. They can inhibit each other.

One of these brains we have in common with all mammals. Let us call it the primitive brain or, rather, the subcortical nervous system, to indicate that it also includes the so-called 'reptilian' structures. The primitive brain cannot be dissociated from the basic adaptive systems, that is to say, the hormonal and immune systems. Emotions and instincts are linked to the activity of the primitive brain.

The other brain can be called the rational brain or neocortex. It is the gigantic development of the rational brain that makes human beings special. It is a kind of supercomputer able to collect, put together, associate and store data brought by the sensory organs. It seems that the right side of the neocortex is usually more directly in touch with the primitive brain.

There are circumstances in which the primitive brain can inhibit the rational one. This is what happens, for example, when a student is paralysed by fear on the day of an exam. Fear can reduce the ability to follow a logical line of reasoning. On the other hand, there are many circumstances in which it is the rational brain that tends to inhibit the primitive one. For example, during an episode of the sexual life such as a delivery, it is the primitive brain that is active. It has to secrete the hormones necessary for the normal progress of the birth. But this involuntary process can be inhibited by an overactive rational brain.

It is because the emotions-instincts are constantly controlled, repressed, inhibited and hidden that they are so difficult to study in humans. The emotions are not studied by those who study the instincts, and vice versa. This trend causes many misunderstandings. For the most part, emotions have been studied by specialists of the nervous system such as N. B. Cannon, J. W. Papez and J. Panksepp; by psychologists; and by philosophers such as William James and Jean-Paul Sartre. Instincts, on the other hand, have been studied primarily by observers of animal behaviour such as Konrad Lorenz and N. Tinbergen.

The following descriptions of some typical situations may throw light on the artificiality of the frontiers between emotion and instinct.

Imagine that an individual suddenly has to face a frightening and threatening giant. Several immediate reactions are possible. The individual might run away. This reaction is similar to that of a rabbit facing a gun-dog. If the individual is himself a giant, aware of his own strength, his immediate reaction might be to stand and fight. This reaction is similar to that of a stag attacked by a wolf. If the individual can neither flee nor fight, he is in a hopeless predicament. There is no choice but to submit. This is the situation of a fawn facing a pack of starving wolves. The individual may also have to face a frightening giant who, after a while, decides to go away. This is the situation of an ass seeing a lion passing by.

These four reactions are instantaneous responses to immediate threats. In each case the brain structures involved are primitive ones, as old as mammals if we consider the history of life on earth; old also if we consider the development of the individual.

The first two examples would most concern those who study behaviour – the so-called ethologists. The cases of the rabbit running away or the stag fighting demonstrate the instincts of flight or fight. The third situation largely concerns the physiologists, who use terms such as 'helplessness' or 'fear paralysis reflex'. It is as if the hopeless individual starts destroying himself by secreting high levels of hormones such as cortisol and endorphins. The fourth situation chiefly concerns philosophers, psychologists and some neurologists, who have a special interest in the emotions in general.

Yet all these specialists, without any reluctance, use the word 'fear' to express what is felt by an ass seeing a lion passing by, or a mouse smelling the odour of a cat, or a human being threatened by a revolver. They do not doubt that these experiences are similar, whether they study the circuit of fear in the brain, the effects of hormones such as adrenalin or what a human being has to say about his feelings.

These examples show that our vocabulary is not adapted to a modern understanding of emotions-instincts. The word 'emotion' is more commonly used by those who are concerned with what is felt. The word 'instinct' is more usually used by those who observe behaviour. This is an oversimplification. Everybody accepts the concept of the expression of emotions, that is to say, behaviour you cannot dissociate from emotions. The expression of fear, for example, is a warning signal, a way to alert others to a possible danger. On the other hand, psychologists study the feelings associated with repressed or sublimated instincts.

Nowadays there is an urgent need to review our vocabulary. *We need a new expression that embraces the concepts of emotion and instinct* to convey the activity of the primitive brain.

Since we have understood the duality of the human brain, we have been in search of a 'phylogenetic' or 'ontogenetic' definition of emotions-instincts, a definition that is based on the age of the structures involved. At the same time we seek a definition that disregards the artificial demarcation between the two words. The frontiers between emotions and instincts are maintained by the limitations imposed by different approaches or disciplines. We are prisoners of vocabulary.

The word 'instinct' is a difficult term to use for many reasons, one being that its definition has long been based upon the distinction between innate and acquired characteristics. The difficulties are extreme where man is concerned, because his main characteristic is the innate ability to make acquisitions, that is to say, to learn! Use of the word 'instinct' is also difficult, because the behaviour and the aim are often mixed up. By instinct, a rabbit starts running when it sees a dog. When talking about the 'flight instinct' as we have done, we imply the end result instead of just describing the phenomenon.

With the word 'emotion' there are other kinds of difficulty. This term often has magical connotations, as if the field of emotion were outside the field of the biological processes. I am often amazed when reading the most serious scientific or medical literature at how many authors oppose 'the emotional level' and 'the physical level', or the 'emotions' and 'the body'. When we analyse an emotion such as fear, with its particular hormonal balance, and the effects of adrenalin on the size of the pupils, the direction of the hair and the heart rate, we are simply studying a physiological process, that is to say, an aspect of life. The emotion of fear is no more magical than any other physiological process or than life in general – it is part of it.

The magical connotations associated with the word 'emotion' are often linked with definitions that use the word 'consciousness'. This makes things still more complicated for phenomena that concern both man and animals. The scientists at the end of the nineteenth century, following Charles Bell and Darwin, carefully avoided these difficulties by studying just the expression of emotions, going into all the details regarding the way the small muscles of the face work when expressing joy, fear, anxiety, etc.

Conjuring up a phrase that embodies the whole field of emotions-instincts and that is based on the age of the brain structures involved has another difficulty attached. Most of the scientists concerned with the physiology of emotions are specialists of the brain, with the majority focused on the emotive circuits of the brain. But today all the boundaries between the primitive brain, the hormonal system and the immune system are obsolete.

The Primal Adaptive System

We need new words to refer to this system, this network that can be clearly seen when old barriers are broken down. Our present vocabulary is not adapted to the enormous quantity of recent data that makes established boundaries embarrassing. Scientists have had to create new disciplines with longer and longer names such as 'psycho-neuro-endocrinology', 'psycho-neuro-immunology' or 'immuno-endocrinology'. I have read about the 'psycho-neuro-immuno-endocrinologic system'! A few examples are enough to demonstrate that there is one big network that transcends the frontiers between primitive brain, hormonal system and immune system. This network needs to be called by a simple name.

Everybody knows about lymphocytes: those cells that are commonly considered to be a part of the immune system. The membrane of some of these cells can secrete hormones such as ACTH and endorphins, as well as having receptors to these hormones. So one can now claim that lymphocytes are also part of the hormonal system. Furthermore, the membrane of lymphocytes can secrete most of the mediators used by the brain cells, and has receptors for them. So lymphocytes might also be integrated into the nervous system.

The hypothalamus is part of the primitive brain and is made up of nerve cells that communicate with other nerve cells by direct contact. But the hypothalamus is also a gland whose secretions regulate the activity of all the other endocrin glands. In return these glands regulate the hypothalamic secretions by a feedback mechanism.

The brain itself is now considered as a gland. It can use the hormonal route, that is to say, chemical messengers, to send information from one part of itself to another. That is why brain grafts can compensate for certain deficiencies, and why some behaviour patterns can be triggered by injecting specific hormones in particular zones of the brain.

Insulin is a hormone secreted by the pancreas. It is also a mediator secreted by cells in the brain and some brain cells have receptors to it.

Nowadays the immune system can be conditioned in the same way that Pavlov conditioned the secretions of a dog's stomach.

Some monocytes – cells of the immune system that occur in the bone marrow – can enter the brain where they are transformed into glial cells. Their role is not well understood.

These few examples, selected from many, are sufficient to demonstrate that there is one unique system, one network I shall call the 'primal adaptive system' – 'primal' because of its early development and maturity, and because it encompasses the adaptive systems that are essential for the survival of the individual and of the species.

When the primal adaptive system goes into action, it can be said that a 'primal adaptive process' occurs. So the primal adaptive process embraces the field of emotion-instinct. This phrase refers to events; it is synonymous with neither 'instinct' nor 'emotion', and it smashes the artificial barriers between these two words.

It is difficult to classify processes such as giving birth or mating with the current vocabulary. As long as there are frontiers between emotions and instincts, one has to use long circumlocutions, saying, for example, that giving birth 'is an involuntary process, an instinctive process that is accompanied by a complex mixture of emotions'. This does not mean that the words 'instinct' and 'emotion' are obsolete. Even if these words are not clear enough for a theoretical or scientific language, they are necessary in everyday life. It will be even easier for me to use them now, having explained the meaning I give to them.

One advantage of the phrase 'primal adaptive process' is the implication that any event of the primal adaptive system at the same time involves the nervous system, a shift of behaviour, a subjective experience, a movement along the pleasure–pain axis, a new hormonal balance, and a change in the working of the immune system. The phrase implies that when we are joyful, for example, the hormonal balance is not the same as when we are sad, and the cells of the immune system do not work in the same way. As for the word 'health', it concerns the quality of the responses of the primal adaptive system.

It is essential to understand that these new definitions, these new visions, are based on the age of the physiological systems involved. In the context of the primal adaptive processes, it is possible to include physiological reactions of self-destruction that may be triggered by situations of hopelessness or helplessness. It is now well understood that living beings have a capacity for self-destruction even at the cell level. By another route, Freud came to the same conclusion and introduced the concept of the death instinct. The postulation of an innately destructive instinct (which includes an auto-destructive instinct) came late in the work of Freud, after the First World War, with the publication of *Beyond the Pleasure Principle* – that is to say, after celebrating the triumph of the libido theory. The status of the death instinct remains unclear within psychoanalytic thought today. However, the theory of death instinct ceases to be purely speculative with our modern understanding of the physiological mechanisms of self-destruction.

Rediscovering Human Instincts

Adapting the language and introducing new theoretical visions are necessary stages in challenging those who deny the reality of human instincts. Humans have at their disposal all the brain structures of other mammals, so it would be amazing if they had completely eliminated the behaviour that is controlled by these structures.

I sensed the importance of these questions watching babies who knew how to find the breast during the first hour after birth, and also seeing their mothers, especially those who had not planned to breast-feed, who immediately knew exactly what had to be done to help the baby suck. Thanks to such scenes, one can understand that instincts are part of human potential. But they are fragile, because they are constantly inhibited, repressed, controlled, altered, and therefore hidden on account of the neocortex's power. But in certain circumstances, they emerge in their entirety. During the hour following birth, the baby, whose neocortex is not yet mature, can already express this complex searching behaviour, modestly called the 'rooting reflex'. In the same way, some mothers, when they are in an atmosphere of complete privacy after a spontaneous birth, are still in such a state of consciousness that they are able to forget everything, even that they had no intention of breast-feeding. They can make the exact gesture that facilitates early sucking. Kittie Frantz, a well-known leader of the La Lèche League, a breast-feeding adviser, spent many years helping young mothers who had difficulties in breast-feeding. After years and years of observation and analysis of attitudes, she understood how some positions, some gestures, some ways to place the hands, could make sucking easier. She told me that she had had the opportunity to watch a film made at the Pithiviers Hospital. A short time after a birth, a young mother, still on another planet, took the baby in her arms and within seconds found all the details of position the breast-feeding counsellors had discovered after years of careful study. After such a story, how can you doubt that humans have instincts, a *savoir-faire* that is guided by the primitive structures of the brain? This shows itself to the full only when the rational brain is at rest, or when the primitive brain is strong enough to be beyond control. This is called the release of inhibitions.

Some other human behaviour is more difficult to interpret. So it is, for example, with behaviour that reminds us of the nesting instinct. In different ways according to the species, all animals prepare the place where the offspring will be welcomed. Even some mammals, such as the dormouse, build nests. Although it is not common to claim that humans have a nesting instinct, careful observation may detect traces of this trait. The behaviour of some women at the end of their pregnancy is sometimes considered to be confusing by the professional obstetricians. In some cases, it might be a subtle expression of the nesting instinct.

In Western societies, many women are encouraged early in pregnancy to make choices about the place of birth. State hospital? Private hospital? Big obstetrics department? Small birthing centre? Home? They usually make such choices after talking to their friends or their doctor, or after reading some books or magazines. Some women unexpectedly sweep aside their earlier choices just before the birth, as if following a sudden inspiration. This is the time they think of home birth, even if they know that such a project cannot be achieved in practice. Such behaviour could be considered inconsistent, unless a connection with the nesting instinct is made. A correct interpretation can avert the danger of a premature choice. To decide where to give birth in the middle of the pregnancy is an intellectual process; it would be much better at this stage to keep the options open and not to preconceive the scenario of the birth.

The need of labouring women to hide or isolate themselves can be regarded as an aspect of the nesting instinct. It is not recognized nowadays, because it is incompatible with the priorities of obstetrics. It comes back in a subtle way when the mother-to-be locks herself in the toilet. It is easier to make the connection with the nesting instinct when a woman suddenly needs to set her cupboards in order or to do the spring cleaning shortly before the labour starts, or even during labour. A young woman called me one afternoon at her home when she felt that the labour was starting. When I arrived, I heard the noise of a vacuum cleaner. Between the contractions she was cleaning. She did not usually do the housework in the afternoon, but on that day it was a kind of need.

The denial of human instincts has serious consequences. It leads to neglect in the development of some aspects of potential. It results in a lack of confidence in some abilities that our species possesses. In a society that ignores instincts, all the aspects of sexual life are made difficult because they are rationalized, planned, controlled. There is a lack of interest in what might be called the development of the emotional life, and attention is turned only towards the development of the intellect.

It is indeed a distinctive feature of human beings, with their strongly developed neocortex, to align their knowledge, their *savoir-faire*, their beliefs, their tastes, and thereby to create cultures. The role of culture is to control, to channel the instincts. But when the instincts are channelled, altered and repressed, it does not mean that they are denied. There is a big difference between channelling the instincts of children, adolescents or adults and preventing the power of instinct from developing at the age when the primal adaptive system is reaching maturity.

One advantage of a definition based on the age of the physiological structures involved is that it indicates in which period of life the emotional and instinctive capacities develop. One can say that the different parts of the primal adaptive system are mature when the baby becomes a child. In other words, they develop during a period I call the 'primal period' and that includes life in the womb, the period of birth and breast-feeding. It is the time when the human being is totally dependent on his mother.

Another advantage of such a definition is to stress that the development of the primitive brain occurs mostly in the womb, that is to say, in water. If one accepts the hypothesis that the huge human neocortex emerged from an aquatic episode in our evolution, one can guess the multiple roots of our special relationship to water. One can claim, from an evolutionary viewpoint, that our neocortex also developed in water. So water appears to be the link between our two brains, the ideal facilitator that can make their coexistence fruitful. In other words, the healing factor *Homo demens* needs.

CHAPTER 11
Homo sapiens

The man who will refrain from disturbing the cycle of water, the man who will curb the destruction of forests, the sexual man who will feel committed to the future, will deserve the name *Homo sapiens*.

Since the emotional desert in man creates the desert in nature, the question is how to enrich the emotional-instinctive power of the man of the future.

With the Help of Science

Modern science can provide an answer – the science that is aware of how early the brain of emotions and instincts matures, and of how the emotional-instinctive power develops when the human baby is dependent on his mother. *One must perceive the link between the baby–mother relationship and that of humanity and mother-earth.*

We have emphasized the conflicts between the primitive brain and the rational brain when referring to our congeneric hominids, *Homo demens*. However, we acknowledge water as a feminine symbol, as the symbol of the mother, and are thus also aware of the possibility of harmonious collaboration between the two brains.

When we seek the help of science to reinforce the emotional-instinctive power of human beings, in so doing we exemplify a possible collaboration, some mutual aid between the rational man and the emotional man. We are reaching a stage in our evolution when we can use science, that is to say our neocortex, to rediscover and reinforce our instincts, in other words, the need to survive.

I will give just one example to indicate the way in which we can rediscover our instincts. We now have enough data to be absolutely convinced of the irreplaceable value of the breast secretions that come before the milk, and in particular the colostrum in the very first hours after birth. The characteristics of colostrum are already less specific on the second day. During the first hours it contains quantities of antibodies that were unsuspected twenty years ago. There is an incredible concentration of the so-called 'IgA' – the antibodies that protect the mucous membranes, and in particular the intestinal mucosa. There are also more of the so-called 'IgG' and 'IgM' on the first day than on the following days.

There are cells in the colostrum with immune action such as macrophages and different kinds of lymphocytes. While they are counted by the million on the first day, they are counted only in thousands by the tenth day. The same is true of the fatty acids, anti-infectious substances and growth factors.

It is also well known that the digestive tract is sterile at birth. Twenty-four hours later, there are five billion living bacteria for every gram of intestinal content. If the baby has ingested colostrum in the first hours after birth, the intestinal flora will be dominated by bifidobacterium, by which we mean germs that protect against dangerous bacteria. It is easy to understand that germs that take possession of the intestinal milieu at the outset will be master of the place and control the settling of other germs. This might have consequences throughout a whole life.

There is now no doubt about the exceptional properties of colostrum during the first hours after birth. One also knows that the human baby is apparently programmed to search immediately for the nipple, and that, immediately after a birth in privacy, some mothers have a reinforced ability to give the breast. Put all these facts together and one is forced to conclude that there is no reason to separate mother and baby during the hours following birth. There is no reason to impose any kind of restriction on the beginning of breast-feeding. The instinct that leads the baby towards the nipple soon after birth, and the instinct that urges the mother to hold the baby close to her breast, must be taken seriously.

Most cultures have always sought to separate mother and new-born baby and to prevent, or even forbid, the taking of colostrum. In some Indian cultures, colostrum was even considered to be bad milk. Two centuries before Christ, Ayuverdic medicine recommended honey and clarified butter for the new-born's first four days, while colostrum was expressed and discarded. This belief in the danger of colostrum was shared by many cultures where the babies were purged and often fed at the beginning by different kinds of surrogate mothers or wet nurses.

In Japan, the elixir *jumigokoto* was given to the new-born for the first three days. Made from a variety of roots and herbs, its ingredients were ritually determined by caste. In the Old Testament, honey and oil are mentioned as food for the new-born.

In traditional Brittany, the rule was not to give the breast before baptism, which did not take place until several days after birth. According to a local popular belief, feeding the baby before baptism would introduce the devil at the same time as the milk.

Greek and Roman physicians unquestioningly recommended delay in first sucking. So did European doctors until the eighteenth century, when the British practitioner William Cadogan spoke highly of colostrum. He was, in fact, sharing the obsession of his predecessors to cleanse the child of 'its long-hoarded excrement'. It is precisely because the mother's first milk was purgative that he questioned the universally well-established dogma. But the result was that neonatal mortality in the UK was reduced by 16 per cent by the end of the century, and this can be attributed to a shift of beliefs regarding colostrum.

Today in many Third World countries millions of babies are deprived of colostrum because of the conviction that it is bad, similar to pus, or a kind of poison. This belief exists in countries thousands of miles apart: for example, among the Indians of Guatemala, Africans in Sierra Leone, Lesotho or Afghanistan, where the new-born is purged with different kinds of herbs and seeds. These facts are especially surprising as the vital importance of colostrum is recognized for animals! The breeders of race-horses know that the taking of colostrum by the new-born foal is essential for the development of its future physical potential.

Colostrum is indeed still more important among mammals, whose placenta is less permeable to the mother's antibodies.

The Maoris, a traditional peasant society, were among the exceptions in their attitude to colostrum, and breast-fed their babies from the first day.

However, the widespread aversion to colostrum is the best possible way to demonstrate what all these cultures have in common up to now. Most cultures tend to control the instincts by weakening them as early as possible. Most cultures tend to reduce the privacy the mother needs to give birth and to alter her instinctive capacity to protect her baby. Most cultures tend to impose pathogenic procedures on helpless new-born babies: separation from the mother; tight swaddling clothes; baptism in cold water; invasive medical practices . . . From this point of view, Tcharkovsky is a man of the past: by training new-born babies, by conditioning them, and by taking them to the limits of pain and endurance.

The body of opinion about colostrum helps us to understand how science might guide human beings in rediscovering their instincts. It is this collaboration between the two brains, the combination of two ways of 'knowing', that brings the hope that a new man might emerge: a man with a strong instinctive potential, with a strong sexuality, committed to the future, and anxious about the evolution of the species. The human condition will stop being a state to undergo and will become a wisdom to acquire.

The authentic *Homo sapiens* will not fear to *develop* the animal inside himself. The development of the whole instinctive and emotional power during infancy should not be confused with an uncontrolled expression of emotions and instincts when man is a child, or an adolescent, or an adult. One cannot imagine human societies without any kind of control over both aggression and the capacity to love, which are so closely connected in the building of a personality. Nor will *Homo sapiens* fear to *communicate* with the animal inside. Easy communication between the rational brain and the primitive, emotional-instinctive brain is considered to be a feminine attribute. Modern science is only now beginning to provide an interpretation of what is commonly called feminine intuition. The bridge – called the corpus callosum – between the right and left hemispheres is 40 per cent larger in the female brain than in the male. In other words, the communication between right and left sides is easier for a woman, and this probably facilitates communication between the rational brain and the primitive, emotional-instinctive one. Slow communication between the rational brain and the emotional one can be an advantage for the human male in some circumstances. Warriors and hunters, for example, can easily kill without being paralysed by feelings of guilt or other forms of inhibiting emotions. But it becomes dangerous at the level of a male-dominated society, in the patriarchal society that has been dominating the planet for thousands of years. It becomes dangerous in a society where the model is masculine, that is to say, in a society where women must express specifically masculine qualities to be successful.

The emergence of an authentic *Homo sapiens* goes hand in hand with the re-emergence of masculine–feminine bipolarity. It implies 'the return of the goddess'. The frustrations imposed upon the new-born baby, the violence he has to undergo such as circumcision, had a reason, or a meaning at a time when the watchword was for humans to dominate the planet and master all the animal and plant species. In the game of selection between species, or the contest between civilizations, the winners were those who knew the best way to develop their potential for aggression. Today the focus is different. The priority is to call a halt to the destruction of our planet. The authentic *Homo sapiens* will create a context of communication, of co-operation, of mutual respect, inside himself and between living species. One must bear in mind that the concept of inter-species communication was introduced by those who believe that dolphins will teach us our true place among all living creatures. The time has come for man to get rid of his 'specism'.

Towards the Ocean

The authentic *Homo sapiens* will turn more and more towards the water, the sea, the ocean. He will look to the element as a feminine symbol – water as a symbol and sexuality cannot be dissociated – and this will help him to become reintegrated into nature.

He will also turn his attention towards water in the search for new sources of energy. He will be inspired by the process of photosynthesis that plants have used for billions of years. He will try to meet the challenge of solar hydrogen, and split water into hydrogen and oxygen by electrolysis. Water might become the fuel of the future. And if one day we learn how to fuse the nuclei of two types of hydrogen, it will be another chapter in the story of hydrogen, which is a component part of water.

Man will turn also towards the ocean to bring to an end the burning of the planet. He will learn to master the infinite energy oceans can offer to man. Can he do that without making the ocean a new colony? Can he do that and maintain the ocean as a respected universe?

The energy of tides is transmitted from the moon to the earth as a result of the gravitational forces at work from the moon's tendency to be pushed away from the earth. The idea of exploiting the energy of tides is not new. The Egyptians had considered this possibility. Later on, the British and the French built tide mills, such as the one at London Bridge, which was in use from the sixteenth to the nineteenth centuries as well as that on the estuary of La Rance in France. In its most rudimentary form a tide mill is composed of a sea wall or barrage blocking the access to an estuary, which houses sluice gates and turbines. At flood-tide the gates are open; at ebb tide, enough water having accumulated, this reservoir is used to operate the turbines. The energy of tides can be used more easily in estuaries, where the height of the tide is more than four metres. There are already such devices at La Rance, at Kislaya Guba in the USSR and at Jiangxia in China. There are many new projects in places such as the estuary of the Severn in the UK and the Bay of Fundy in Canada, where the tide is sixteen metres high (the highest in the world) and where computer simulations have shown that a tidal power would raise the tide levels as far away as Boston. The models can now be used to assess the environmental economic cost of tidal power. One must keep in mind that the conditions that make an estuary ideal for generating power also make it a rich intertidal feeding area for birds. Also the barrage could lead to an accumulation of pollutants. A tide mill can be maintained for a long time. A sluice gate can operate effectively for more than a century, and the turbines can be periodically renovated. The use of the energy of tides might become important in some particular areas, and the power plants need not be large.

As for wave power, it comes from the energy of the sun, since waves are created by the effect of the wind on the surface of the sea, and winds are caused by the sun. Waves can travel thousands of miles. In the North Atlantic wave power is evaluated at 10 Kw per square metre. Reports by some experts suggest that the electricity generated by waves would be less expensive to produce than the energy derived from petroleum and, after huge investments, easy to recoup. This process has great potential in many areas, with the exception of the tropics.

The use of thermal energy of the seas is based upon the difference in temperature between the surface and deep water. This is not a new idea, since it was proposed by Jacques d'Arsonval in 1881. The potential of this source of energy is enormous. It is easy to exploit it when the difference of temperature between the surface water and the water at 1,000 metres is 18°C or more. The most promising zones for this process are in the western Pacific.

Harnessing the thermal energy of the seas requires technology on a massive scale. A by-product of the process might be supplies of fresh water, and the deep water might be used for fish breeding. The ecological effects of the displacement of water will have to be evaluated. Theoretically it could be a way to provide the tropical countries with a cheap source of energy in almost unlimited quantities.

*

Homo sapiens will not only turn towards the oceans in search of energy and food but will also regard them as the matrix of all living creatures. He will turn towards the ocean to see the water, the most powerful, the most deeply rooted of all his symbols. And this symbol is feminine. It implies that we belong to a sexed (not neutered), bipolar world. But at the beginning was the feminine.

The ocean provides *Homo sapiens* with a focus for the re-discovery of the central metaphor of an old and forgotten wisdom. It is the vision of the ocean where every wave, apparently distinct, is intrinsic to the whole. Every being is a temporary and fleeting form that is absorbed in an amorphous and unlimited whole.

'The sage who wants to change the world will have to look towards the water,' said the Taoist Tchouang-Tsu. The sage who wants to change the world must look at the new-born baby. 'Civilization will commence on the day when the well-being of the new-born baby prevails over any other consideration,' said Wilhelm Reich. Let us combine these two prophecies at a time when the advent of an authentic *Homo sapiens* is the only chance for the planet to survive. May such wisdom, such sapience, be the prime accomplishment of man.

SELECT BIBLIOGRAPHY

Chapter 1: How to Use Water During Labour
Michel Odent, *Birth Reborn* (Pantheon, New York, 1984)
Erik Sindenbladh, *Vatterbarn* (Akademilitteratur AB, Stockholm, 1982)

Chapter 2: Interpretations
N. Newton, 'The Foetus Ejection Reflex Revisited', *Birth*, vol. 14 (1987), pp. 106–8
Michel Odent, 'Birth Under Water', *Lancet* (24 December 1983), pp. 1476–7
Michel Odent, 'The Foetus Ejection Reflex', *Birth*, vol. 14 (1987), pp. 104–5
Catherine Tchobroutsky, 'Le Premier cri', *La Recherche*, vol. 6, no. 61 (November 1975), pp. 933–8
'Vestibular Function in Microgravity', editorial in the *Lancet* (8 September 1984), p. 961

Chapter 3: The Power of Water
F. Leboyer, *Birth without Violence* (Wildwood House, Aldershot, 1975)
Michel Odent, *Genèse de l'homme écologique* (Epi, Paris, 1979)
Michel Odent, *Entering the World* (Marion Boyars, London, 1984)
Sondra Ray, *Ideal Birth* (Celestial Arts, Millbrae, California, 1985)
Rima Beth Star, *The Healing Power of Birth* (Star Publishing, Austin, Texas, 1986)

Chapter 4: The Erotic Power of Water
Gaston Bachelard, *L'eau et les rêves* (José Corti, Paris, 1942)
Gwen Benwell and Arthur Waugh, *Sea Enchantress* (Hutchinson, London, 1961)
Sandor Ferenczi, *Thalassa* (H. Karnac, London, 1989)
Shere Hite, *The Hite Report* (Macmillan, New York, 1976)

Ivan Illich, *H₂O and the Waters of Forgetfulness* (Marion Boyars, London, 1986)

Helen S. Kaplan, *The New Sex Therapy* (Brunner-Mazel, New York, 1974)

W. Masters and V. Johnson, *Human Sexual Response* (Little, Brown, Boston, 1966)

W. Masters and V. Johnson, *Human Sexual Inadequacy* (Little, Brown, Boston, 1970)

Pomeroy Wardell, *Dr Kinsey and the Institute for Health Research* (New American Library, New York, 1972)

Glenn Wilson, *The Secrets of Sexual Fantasy* (Dent, London, 1978)

Chapter 5: The Tao of Medicine

Eileen Herzberg, *Reborn with the Swimming Shrink, Independent* (13 December 1988)

Sheila Kitzinger, *Women's Experience of Sex* (Dorling Kindersley, London, 1983)

Charleville-Mézières, 'L'eau et la relation', *Comptes rendus du colloque* (10 January 1987)

'Le quotidien du médecin', *Dossier le médecin et la mer*, no. 2926 (25 April 1983)

J. O'Hare, *et al.*, 'Observations on the Effects of Immersion in Bath Spa Water', *British Medical Journal*, vol. 291 (21–8 December 1985), pp. 1747–51

Davis Watts, 'Hot Springs Business Booms', *The Times* (6 March 1987)

Chapter 6: Religion

Jacques Benveniste, *et al.*, 'Human Basophile Degranulation Triggered by Anti-serum against IgE', *Nature*, vol. 333 (30 June 1988)

Scholem Gershon, *On the Kabbalah and Its Symbolism* (Routledge & Kegan Paul, London, 1965)

C. L. Kervan, 'Transmutations biologiques', *Le courrier du livre* (1966)

R. Lawrence, *Christian Healing Rediscovered* (Kingsway, Eastbourne, 1976)

'L'homme et l'eau', *Co évolution* no. 10 (Autumn 1982)

Stephen Parsons, *The Challenge of Christian Healing* (SPCK, London, 1986)

Theodor Schwenk, *Sensitive Chaos* (Schocken Books, New York, 1976)

Chapter 7: Man and Dolphin

B. Arensburg, *et al*., 'A Middle Palaeolithic Human Hyoid Bone', *Nature* vol. 33 (27 April 1989), pp. 758–60

W. Booth, 'The Social Lives of Dolphins', *Science*, vol. 240 (1988), pp. 1273–4

G. H. Bourne (ed.), *The Chimpanzee: Anatomy, Behaviour and Diseases* (Karger, Basel, 1969)

Charles Darwin, *Descent of Man* (Random House, New York, 1871)

D. Denton, *The Hunger for Salt* (Springer Verlag, New York, 1982)

F. De Waal, 'La réconciliation chez les primates', *La Recherche*, no. 210 (May 1989)

Jan Golab, 'To the Sea in Hopes', *Western's World* (July 1985)

Terry Hankins, 'Biologically Speaking', *Dolphin Dialogue*, vol. 1, no. 3 (Key Largo, Florida)

Alister Hardy, 'Was Man More Aquatic in the Past?', *New Scientist*, vol. 7 (April 1960), pp. 642–5

L. Kruger, 'The Thalamus of the Dolphin in Comparison with Other Mammals', *Journal of Comparative Neurology*, vol. 111, pp. 133–94

Elaine Morgan, *The Aquatic Ape* (Souvenir Press, London, 1982)

Elaine Morgan and M. Verhaegen, 'In the Beginning was the Water', *New Scientist* (6 March 1986), pp. 62–3

Desmond Morris, *The Naked Ape* (Jonathan Cape, London, 1967)

François Xavier Pelletier, *Ballade pour un dauphin sacré* (Arthaud, Paris, 1988)

Win Wenger, *How to Increase Your Intelligence* (United Educational Services, East Aurora, NY, 1988)

Warren Zapol, 'Diving Adaptations of the Weddell Seal', *Scientific American* (June 1987), pp. 80–85

Chapter 8: Homo aquaticus

William Calvin, 'The River that Flows Uphill' (Sierra Club Books, San Francisco, 1986)

P. Choukroune, *et al*., 'Tectonics of the Westernmost Gulf of Aden and the Gulf of Tadjoura from Submersible Observations', *Nature*, vol. 319 (30 January 1986), pp. 396–9

Jacques Cousteau, *The Ocean World of Jacques Cousteau: Mammals in the Sea* (Angus & Robertson, London, 1980)

Charles Darwin, *On the Origin of Species* (Collins, London, 1859)

E. Delson, 'Oreopithecus is a Cercopithecoid After All' *American Journal of Physical Anthropology*, vol. 50, no. 3 (1979), pp. 431–2

Leon La Lumière, 'Danakil Island' in Elaine Morgan, *The Aquatic Ape* (Souvenir Press, London, 1982)

Graham Richards, *Human Evolution* (Routledge & Kegan Paul, London, 1987)

Betsy Smith, 'Project Inreach: A Program to Explore the Ability of Atlantic Bottle-nose Dolphins to Elicit Communication Responses from Autistic Children' in *New Perspectives on Our Lives with Companion Animals* (University of Pennsylvania Press, Philadelphia, 1983)

Betsy Smith, 'Using Dolphins to Elicit Communication from an Autistic Child' in *The Pet Connection* (Center for the Study of Human–Animal Relationships and Environments, Minneapolis, 1984)

Chapter 9: Homo demens

Catherine Caufield, 'Rainforests Face Attack of Double Standards', *New Scientist* (5 June 1986), p. 20

Jeremy Cherfas, 'The Sorry History of Whaling', *New Scientist* (5 June 1986)

Club du Sahel, *CILSS: The Sahel Drought Control and Development Programme 1975–9* (Club du Sahel, Paris, 1981)

Arthur Credland, *Whales and Whaling* (Seven Hills Books, Cincinnati, 1983)

Roger Dadoun, 'Desert' in R. Dadoun, *Cent fleurs pour Wilhelm Reich* (Payot, Paris, 1975)

M. H. Glautz (ed.), *Desertification* (Westview Press, Boulder, Colorado, 1977)

Alain Grainger, *Desertification* (International Institute for Environment and Development, London and Washington, DC, 1982)

P. L. Jaiswal (ed.), *Desertification and Its Control* (Model Press, New Delhi, 1977)

James Jenkins, *History of the Whale Fisheries* (Associated Faculty Press, New York, 1971)

Michel Odent, *Genèse de l'homme écologique* (Epi, Paris, 1979)

Auders Rapp, *A Review of Desertification in Africa*, Secretariat for International Ecology (SIESS, Stockholm, Sweden, 1974)

Allen Rodway, *Conservation and Management of Whales* (Washington State University Press, Pullman, Washington, 1980)

Chapter 10: Outline of a Theory of Emotion-instincts
C. Bell, *The Anatomy and Philosophy of Expression as Connected with the Fine Arts* (H. G. Bohn, London, 1806)

W. B. Cannon, 'The James–Lange Theory of Emotions', *American Journal of Psychology*, vol. 39 (1927), p. 106

Charles Darwin, 'Instinct', in *On the Origin of Species* (Collins, London, 1859)

Charles Darwin, *The Expression of Emotions in Man and Animals* (John Murray, London, 1872)

William James, 'What is Emotion?' *Mind*, vol. 19 (1884), pp. 188–205

Konrad Lorenz, *Vergleichende Verhaltensforschung: Grundlagen der Ethologie* (Springer Verlag, Vienna, 1978)

J. W. Papez, 'A Proposed Mechanism of Emotion', *Archives of Neurology and Psychiatry*, vol. 38 (1937), pp. 725–44

J. Panksepp, 'Toward a General Psychobiological Theory of Emotions', *Behavioral and Brain Sciences*, vol. 5, no. 3 (September 1982)

Jean-Paul Sartre, *The Emotions: Outline of a Theory* (The Philosophical Library, New York, 1948)

N. Tinbergen, *The Study of Instinct* (Oxford University Press, Oxford, 1951)

Chapter 11: Homo sapiens
Naomi Baumslag, 'Breast-feeding: Cultural Practices and Variations' in *Advances in Maternal and Child Health*, vol. 7 (Clarendon Press, Oxford, 1987)

W. Cadogan, 'Essay on Nursing and Management of Children from Birth to Three Years of Age', Letter to the Governor of the Foundling Hospital (1773)

W. D. Davidson, 'A Brief History of Infant Feeding', *Journal of Paediatrics*, vol. 43 (1953), pp. 74–87

Wilhelm Reich, The Murder of Christ (Orgone Institute Press, New York, 1953)

Index

Index

colour of water, 2, 30, 41
cord, umbilical, 12
Cornwall, 23
cortisol, 43, 105
Cousteau, Jacques, 57, 92, 95
Cranach, Lucas, 28
Crawford, Professor Michael, 82
crocodiles, 65, 89
culture: denies instincts, 112, 116
cycle of water, 96–9, 113
Cyprus, 20

Dart, Raymond, 85
Darwin, Charles, 50, 58, 87, 107
David, King of Israel, 23
Davies, Dr P., 75
Dead Sea, 37
Decadence (artistic movement), 29
dehydration, 39
deluge, primeval, 86–9
Delville, J., 29
desertification, 97, 102, 113
Desvallières, Georges, 29
diet, 72–3, 82
disease, 73–6; *see also* medicine
diving, 31, 67–9, 71, 73, 75, 88
dogs, 12
dolphins: abstract thought, 80; and
    autism, 94; brain, 63, 78–9, 81–2;
    communication, 70, 92–3, 94,
    117; hearing, 70, 80; going back
    to sea, 89; intelligence, 81–2;
    killed by pollution, 100; man's
    collaboration with, 19, 92–5,
    117; midwives, 18, 93; senses, 80;
    sexual behaviour, 63;
    Tcharkovsky and, 18, 92–3;

therapy involving, 93–4;
    verticality, 61
Domenico, Gisela Schuback de, 41
dreams, 2, 19, 21, 81
Dubois, Eugène, 84
duck-footed humans, 69, 75–6
dugong, 61, 89

ear, inner, 5, 13
eccrine glands, 60
ecology, 96–102, 117–20
Edwards, Henri Milne-, 12
Egypt, 23, 54, 71, 93, 97, 118
Einstein, Albert, 81
Eipo tribe of New Guinea, 77
ejaculation, 10
elephants, 90
Ellis, Henry Havelock, 31
emotions, 8, 44, 70, 103–12
endangered species, 98, 99
endorphins, 8, 11, 62, 105, 107
energy from oceans, 118–19
environment, man and, 96–102,
    117–20
erogenous zones, 62
eroticism, 22–34, 36
escape, water as way of, 66
Eskimos, 73
Ethiopia, 86–7, 88–9
Euripides (Greek tragedian), 39

fat: blood, 75; subcutaneous, 59, 82
fear, 5, 6–8, 48–9, 104, 105, 106
feet, webbed, 69, 75–6, 90
femininity, 116–17: water as
    symbol of, 35, 113, 117, 119–20
Ferenczi, Dr Sandor, 25–6, 31–2

Index

Index

ritual, 48, 50
rivers, 48, 54–5, 118
Rome, ancient, 36, 44, 67, 93, 97, 115
rooting reflex, 110
Roscoff, Brittany, 39
Rougerie, Jacques, 95
Rusalka (mermaid), 23, 30
Russell, Richard, 39

saccule, 13
salt, 37, 65, 73: glands, 64–5
sand, 41
Sartre, Jean-Paul, 104
Saurel, Anne-Marie, 40–41
Scammon, Captain Charles, 101
Scarr, Dee, 69
Schaffer, Victor, 63
schizophrenia, 40
Schwabe, Carlos, 29
science and instincts, 113–17
Scotland: legends, 23–4
sculpture, 30
sea, 117–20: birth in, 2, 20–21; ecology, 100–102; energy from, 118–19; thalassotherapy, 38–9
sea-lions, 63, 75, 89
sea mammals: absence of hair, 58; birth process, 77; brain size, 82; communication, 70; diving, 67–8, 73; going back to sea, 89; midwives, 77; salt glands, 65; sexual behaviour, 62–3; spine, 61; subcutaneous fat, 59; see also dolphins
seals, 58, 63, 65, 68, 75, 89, 92
sebaceous system, 74

senses, 3, 5, 13, 14, 15, 79–80
Severn estuary, 118
sexual behaviour see intercourse
sexuality, meaning of, xiv
shamanism, 46, 95
shoulder, 74
Siena, Italy, 26
Sinclair, Professor Hugh, 72–3
Sind, Pakistan, 63
sirène, 23
skin, 58, 73, 74, 80
sleep: rapid eye movements, 81
Smirnov, Igor, 54, 67
Smith, Betsy, 94
Smith, Cyril, 53
snakes, 87–8, 89, 91
social structures, 50, 58, 62, 117
Solomon, King of Israel, 97
sound, sensitivity to, 69–72
Spa, Belgium, 36
spas, thermal, 35–8
speech, 67, 70, 71–2, 75
sphere, water re-creates, 54–5
spine, flexibility of, 61, 74
spirituality, 18, 44, 46–7, 80
sports, 66, 69, 73
springs, healing see spas
Strauss, Johann, 30
structure of water, molecular, 52–4
submarines, sightseeing, 69
submission in illness, 43, 44
Sudden Infant Death Syndrome, 74–5
Suez, Gulf of, 92